DEER HUNTING IN OHIO

ROBERT LOEWENDICK

DEER HUNTING IN OHIO

History, Legends & Trophies

The History PRESS

Published by The History Press
Charleston, SC 29403
www.historypress.net

First published 2010

Manufactured in the United States

ISBN 978.1.59629.890.3

Library of Congress Cataloging-in-Publication Data

Loewendick, Robert.
Deer hunting in Ohio : history, legends, and trophies / Robert Loewendick.
p. cm.
Includes bibliographical references.
ISBN 978-1-59629-890-3
1. Deer hunting--Ohio. 2. Deer hunting--Ohio--History. 3. White-tailed deer hunting--Ohio. 4. White-tailed deer hunting--Ohio--History. I. Title.
SK301.L557 2010
799.2'765209771--dc22
2010032454

Thanks to Dad for taking me hunting and to Mom for preparing the meals afterward. And for the love and encouragement I received from both of you every day.

CONTENTS

PREFACE

When I was informed that The History Press was looking for an author to write a book highlighting Ohio's white-tailed deer hunting, multiple thoughts flooded my head at once. Wow, I thought: an opportunity to assemble my home state's history of its deep deer hunting heritage in one publication. I considered it to be an honor, and it has been, to be the writer to do the worthy task. Ohio possesses several outdoor heritages, and deer hunting is certainly near the top of that list. My intent for this book was to entertain and inform deer hunters, deer enthusiasts or anyone interested in learning about one of Ohio's most interesting cultural and economic forces.

As a freelance outdoor writer, I'm blessed with constant and numerous excursions around Ohio in search of outdoor adventures. While I'm tracking down the latest news on the hunting and fishing front, I'm frequently stumbling over bits and pieces of the past—both short- and long-term history. These discoveries often intrigue me and have led to notes scribbled on paper and in memory, some of which are shared on the pages before you. Ohio's deer hunting heritage began before the state was a state. The land at that time was crawling with abundant wildlife, especially white-tailed deer. Because of the lengthy timeline of the deer's existence in Ohio, an abundance of lore also exists. After reading the book from start to finish, you will have experienced a summary of this storied timeline.

While researching material for this project, I met many interesting and colorful characters. I talked with hunters who have racked up decades of hunting stories and experiences. Those hunters had walked the woods when there was not a deer within a hundred miles or more. Some shared stories and some, only opinions. Some gladly told me their names, and some preferred to remain anonymous for various reasons. Although some of the tales shared in this book don't have a named source, the approximate location and interesting facts of the stories do exist. I interviewed middle-aged hunters who revealed their admiration for Ohio's deer hunting and how they became involved. These hunters have a few decades of deer hunting experience that offer a diverse look into the past and current state of deer hunting in Ohio.

I talked deer hunting with hunters, wildlife enthusiasts, wildlife biologists and an archaeologist. What these Ohioans revealed about the state's deer hunting past was a mix of fascinating tales and surprising facts. Together, the information revealed is an accurate insight into one of the Midwest's greatest deer hunting states. I've hunted deer for the last thirty years. I'm not a white-tailed deer hunter extraordinaire by any stretch of the imagination, but a whitetail enthusiast I surely am. Before this book project, I considered myself as having a fair amount of knowledge about Ohio's deer hunting heritage. I did, to an extent. But as I gathered and compiled notes, conducted interviews, pulled out previous notes and recalled past interview conversations, a great story gradually came into view. The result is a walk through Ohio's deer hunting past and into the present. I hope you enjoy reading about the journey as much as I did researching and telling it.

ACKNOWLEDGEMENTS

I offer a sincere thanks to the following people who shared invaluable information and their time with me while researching and writing this book. The Public Information Officers and their administrators of the ODNR, Division of Wildlife (DOW); Vicki Mountz, Jamey Graham, Kathy Garza-Behr, Susie Vance and Vicki Ervin. For photos and historical information, ODNR, DOW Photographer Tim Daniel. For insights to their parts of the state, fellow outdoor writers and members of Outdoor Writers of Ohio; Tom Cross, Larry Moore, Dave Maurer, John Bennett and Judy Wells. For information regarding the management plans that have been so successful in growing Ohio's deer herd, ODNR, DOW Biologists (Active and retired); Mike Tonkovich, Pat Ruble, Dan McMillen and Scott Peters. For sharing their stories about their trophy bucks; Mike Beatty, Brad Jerman and Mike Rex. Retired Wildlife Enforcement Supervisor, Jerry Wade for his stories of behind the badge. For showing me evidence of the earliest deer hunters, Ohio archeologist, Steve House. To my brother Ted Loewendick for helping me find the time to complete the book. To the numerous people who granted me interviews, welcomed me into their home and into their past. All of those interviews, whether noted in the book or not, were used to bring Ohio's deer hunting story to these pages. I fully understand our days on this earth are limited and each one is a gift, so to my wife Linda, daughter Danielle and son Rob, I thank you for your patience and your loving support during this book project and each day we share together.

INTRODUCTION

The November breeze blowing across the ridge top was pleasant; the cooling effect was appreciated, as I was still feeling warm from the hike up the steep hill. I unzipped my camo coat and began to scan the hayfield in front of me. Seeing no deer, I walked into the edge of the thicket surrounding the big wild cherry tree and cleared a spot for me to sit on the ground. There were no sounds on the high, open ridge other than a screeching red-tailed hawk and the light wind rustling the leaves around me. As I nestled into my cleared spot on the ground, I wondered if Dad (now deceased) had gotten himself into his site we had cleared for him the week prior. Dad was a leg amputee, and he used an all-terrain vehicle (ATV) to make the trek to his hunting spot at the bottom of the ridge along a cornfield. Once near his location, he would park the ATV and use a cane to assist his maneuvering into position as he stumbled through the corn stubble. I hoped that he had settled in okay. As a sixteen-year-old boy, I was concerned about him as much as I was about seeing and possibly having a shot at my first white-tailed deer.

As I sat there against the base of the wild cherry, I enjoyed the view before me and the thoughts it provoked. It was the last day of Ohio's 1981 gun season, and I had only seen a few deer earlier in the week. It had been two days since the last deer sighting, and I was beginning to lose confidence that I would end the season with a filled deer tag. Being high on the open ridge gave me a wide-open view of the sky. The clouds slowly moving against their gray background seemed as if they were only a few feet above my head—as if I could reach up and touch them. My eyes settled back down to earth, and the field scanning began once again. I began to visualize a string of deer walking from the mature hardwood forest surrounding the hilltop and walking toward me. The visualization was one I had entertained myself with all week, but it never materialized.

The hilltop overlooked my grandfather's farm, which was now owned by my uncle after my grandfather's passing a decade before my birth. Spending days roaming the hundred acres of woodlands covering the huge Muskingum County hill was often done by myself, siblings and cousins as children. Now the teenage years had brought new pursuits, and deer hunting was one of them. My relatives had hunted our hills and meadows for years prior to my existence, but now it was my time to join the hunters of the family, and I was both excited and proud to do so. My hunting experience to that point had been limited to raccoon, squirrel and rabbit. The deer was my first big game quarry, and I soon realized that it was a different game than previous hunts.

A quick flash of something pouncing up through the field woke me from my daydream. A red fox was working over a field mouse in hopes to make it his meal. The fox's hunt was amusing and provided some entertainment for this deer-less deer hunter. I was impressed by the fox's hunting skills. He was very patient, waiting for the right moment to make his move. After one high jumping pounce, he came up with the rodent in his mouth. He ate the mouse right there and then lied down to process the meal. Another red-tailed hawk, or possibly the same one, flew over the fox, and the two exchanged stares. It was as if the two hunters were saying hello and offering and accepting congratulations.

My mind returned to the days spent hunting the land with cousins and what it must have been like hunting these hills as a settler, moving through the area or settling in and building a homestead. The Licking River courses along the bottomland of my grandfather's farm, and I often wondered what the sight might have been centuries ago with Indians camped along the river's banks. How important the deer and other game must have been to the people who didn't rely on a grocery store for a steady food supply. One deer supplied food, clothing and tools to a culture that was well connected to the natural world. I thought of what it would be like today if our culture was better connected to the natural world.

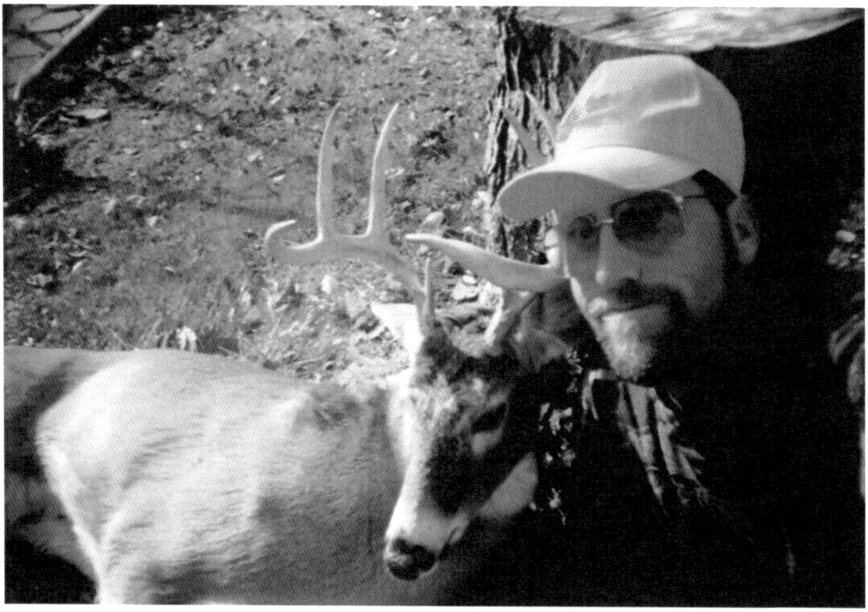

The author took this buck in southeast Ohio in 1998. The author's hunting passion was instilled by his father at an early age. *Robert Loewendick.*

The hawk made a third flyover, but this time it seemed to be looking at me. My blaze orange hat was surely sticking out like a sore thumb in the vision of the bird of prey. I watched the hawk fly away from me and toward the farthest corner of the hayfield. As he soared just over the treetops, something else came into focus. A deer was standing at the forest edge. "A deer!" I whispered to myself. Finally a deer, but I soon realized that it was a long way from me and that the chances of it making its way close enough for a shot were slim. My preseason scouting put me where I was instead of where the deer entered the hayfield this day. I second-guessed my decision to pick the wild cherry location and was looking at a way to stalk the deer that was still feeding and not moving in any one direction. Stalk? I had never stalked anything before. Not a raccoon. Not a squirrel. Not a rabbit. Something was telling me to stay still, but another unseen force was telling me to begin sneaking toward the deer. I turned my focus back to observing the deer when another and then another deer walked out of the woods and joined the first. My heartbeats were increasing.

The deer lined up and began walking and feeding along the field edge. They followed the edge as they continued their slow march around the field.

For thirty minutes they kept the course, slowly getting closer to my corner of the field. I couldn't believe it. Were they really going to keep coming? I had calmed down some since the deers' appearance, but that was soon reversed. The three-deer train made the last turn before they would walk well within shooting range. They kept coming. My breathing was getting faster. Where was Dad? Was he okay? How would he react if he heard me shoot? How would I react if I heard him shoot? The deer were getting closer, and it was time to put the gun into firing position.

The three does were broadside to my position. They were all adults. I had a doe permit. I had dreams of a taking a big buck to hang on my wall, but the does in front of me were all I was thinking about now. I picked out the largest of the three and aimed my old single-shot H&R twenty-gauge. I held my breath and squeezed the trigger. One deer turned and ran full speed in the direction from which they had come. A second deer made a short loop and soon followed the first. Where was the third deer? I thought I heard one run into the woods. The field sloped down in front of me, which made it hard to see exactly where the deer had been standing. I stood slowly so not to spook the missing doe if she was standing in the edge of the woods. She

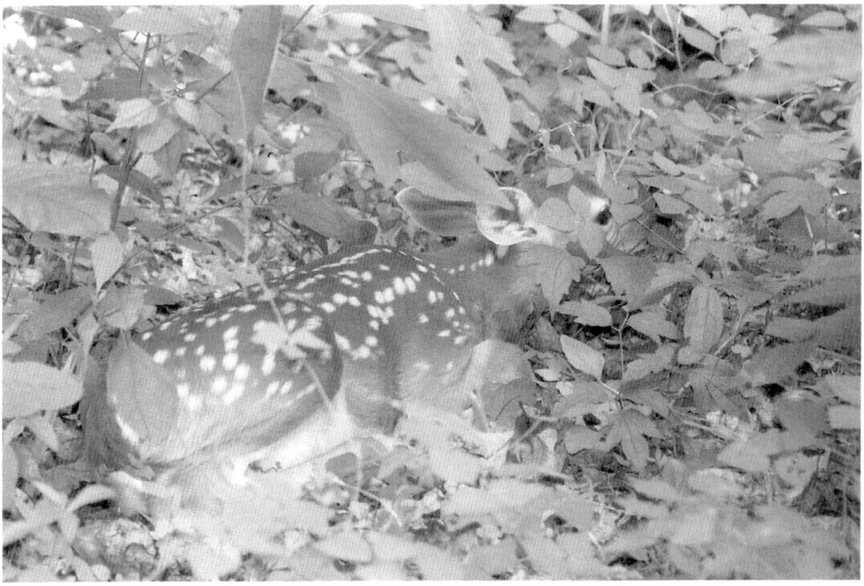

A whitetail's sense of survival begins functioning at birth. *Judy Wells.*

was not in the woods. She was lying in the field where she stood when the rifled slug went through her spine. I had taken my first deer. I field-dressed her, thanked the maker for the gift and trotted off to get Dad.

Ohio's deer hunting heritage is actually centuries old. This book leads the reader through a chronological journey around the state's deer country. As I began the planning stages of researching and writing the book, I decided to draw a line north and south through Columbus and east and west, also through Columbus, which created four quarters to explore and better define Ohio's diverse geography and how deer hunting fits the particular region. Each quarter has experienced deer and deer hunting a bit differently, but some aspects are similar.

To get a real sense of deer hunting in the four regions I conducted interviews with hunters, family members of hunters, retired wildlife officers, retired and active wildlife biologists, an Ohio archaeologist, outdoor writers and photographers, townsfolk, farmers and other private landowners and many individuals sitting on stools or standing with fellow deer hunters at deer checking stations and small-town convenience stores and outdoor gear outfitting stores. Some interviews were recent, and some were completed through the last decade and from deer stories shared with me over the last forty-five years. The result was a realistic and fascinating slice of each region's contribution to Ohio's deer hunting history, heritage and lore.

Chapter 1

OHIO'S EARLY DEER HUNTERS

Native Americans and then Settlers

The Native American teenager ran hard, skirting the small creek as his cousin matched his pace on the other side of the creek. The deer they were pursuing was headed for the river. It had to either swim or turn broadside to offer a shot to either of the two young bowmen. The smell of the fresh soil and covering vegetation being kicked up by the running hunters followed in the air wake turning in the turbulence caused by the hunters. Each time the hunters paused, both to listen for the deer and to catch a refueling breath, the aroma of the summer woodlands' early morning came over them. To be alive and strong this day was respected, as was the possibility of bringing home fresh venison for their tribe.

The boys paused once more, kneeling and listening intently for a sign to advise their next move. Moments passed before one of the hunters saw a brown and then a white patch of hair slowly moving through the heavy brush skirting the river's edge. The arrow being pulled back was as silent as the deer attempting to make an escape unnoticed. The accompanying hunter watched his relative from the corner of his eye, remaining rock still, but inside he was jumping with excitement. The deer stepped into a small clearing of the brush. The arrow was released.

The deer leaped forward and was once again running full speed. But only for a couple of seconds, before the arrow's penetration performed its duty. The flint arrowhead led the exit of life from the swift, prudent and treasured white-tailed deer lying before the two young hunters. They offered thanks

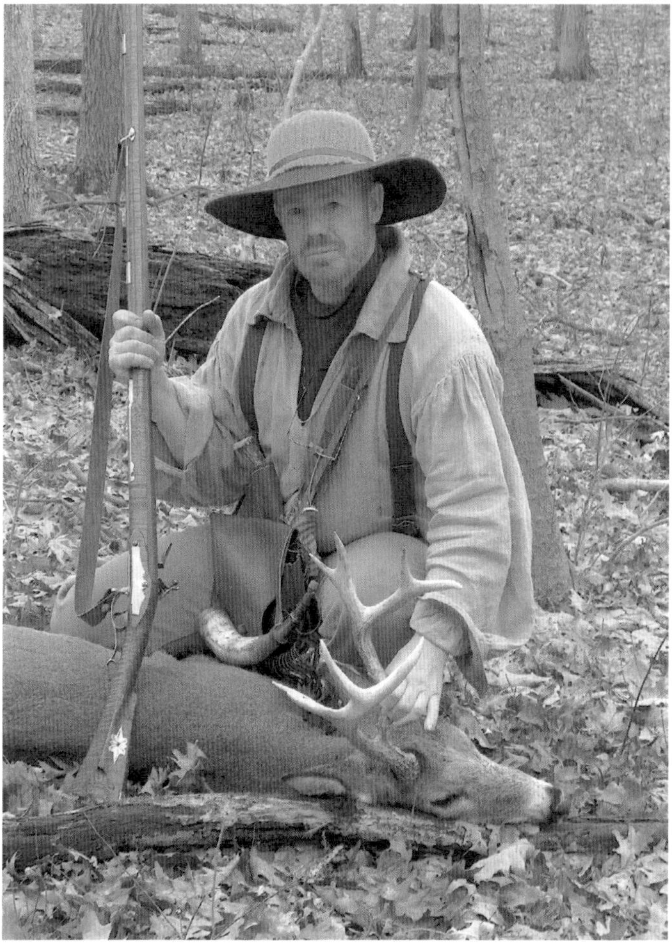

Ohio's early settlers found the white-tailed deer to be a valuable resource for food and trade. *Tom Cross.*

to the power above and hurriedly went to work on preparing the kill for presentation to the tribe. Surely the elders would approve; the experienced warriors, the sustaining hunters of their village and their direct family members would also be proud and thankful for the gift of nourishment. As the boys carried the deer within sight of the village, several small children came running and yelling with excitement. Two older hunters met them and inspected the result of their sunrise hunt. The young hunters received a couple of assuring smiles and positive head nods. The deer was delivered to the elders.

Ohio's Native Americans and the Whitetail

The white-tailed deer has been a valuable asset to the people living in the Ohio region for centuries. As the various Indian tribes interacted with one another, the whitetail was involved in many daily needs and ceremonial practices. Modern archaeological research revealed many deer bones throughout digs across the state, proving that the deer was highly valued for many reasons and for many centuries. Showing appreciation for the numerous uses that one deer provided for several people, deer were an honored creature, as were most wildlife. Although wild game was abundant in the Ohio region for most of the years of the past twenty centuries, the deer was the most sought after, for sustainment of the people and also for commercial advancements and profits into the late 1700s. Many historical tales of the Ohio region include herds of elk and an abundant population of black bears, but the reality is that the deer was the plentiful and popular game animal of those times.

Throughout the Ohio region, but typically more so in the southern half of Ohio, archaeologists have discovered that the admiration for and uses of the deer were the common thread of the Indian culture as early as three thousand years ago. During the exploration of a Hopewell Indian mound in southern Ohio, several deer-themed items were found, one impressive item being an antler effigy made from sheet copper and representing a deer head with antlers. The deer was such an important resource to the early people that the animal was praised during spiritual ceremonies. Similar items honoring the deer also were created and used from 1000 BC to AD 400.

The deer population blossomed in the late 1400s as the Indians also returned to the Ohio region after being absent from the late 1300s. Archaeologists have no carbon-dated materials from that timeline that show there was activity in the region during that time. A devastating drought is the likely and estimated reason. Archaeological digs have turned up deer bones and the many uses that one deer provided. The cut marks or butcher marks left on deer bones by the Indians are evidence of the deer's primary purpose at the time. For example, if the legs were removed at a higher point, close to the torso, then possibly the legs were not as needed as was the remainder of the deer and its hide. If the legs were separated in sections, with butcher marks found on several points along a leg bone, then it is likely that the entire deer was utilized.

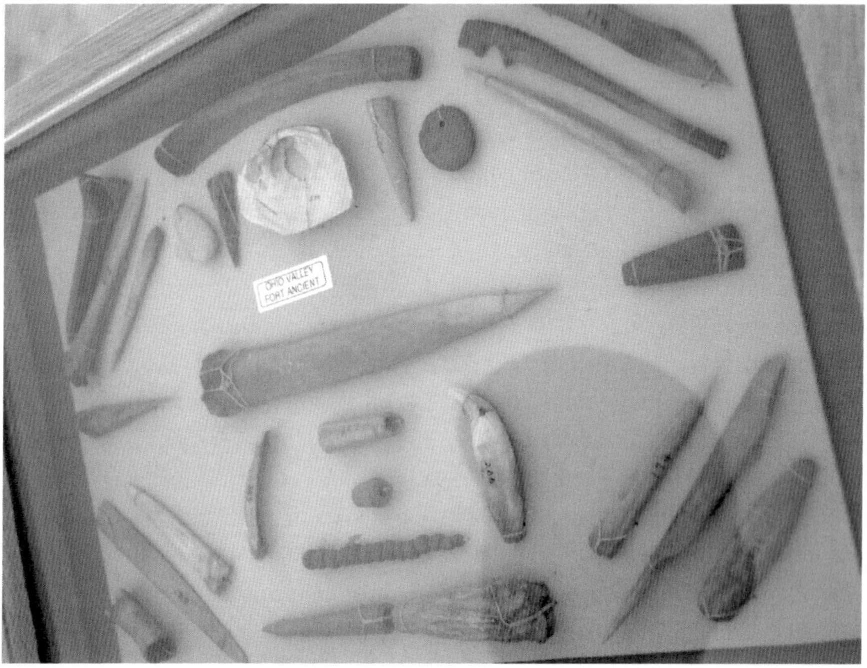

Native Americans utilized nearly every part of a deer's body for a variety of reasons. Even the bones were used for an assortment of tools. *Robert Loewendick.*

A deer was processed for meat and its hide primarily, but its bones were equally as important. The jawbones were used to shell corn and for other uses in harvesting and processing crops. The scapula, or shoulder bone, provided various tools. A scapula lashed to a stick made a fine hoe for managing crop plantings. Needles and awls were also crafted from a deer's scapula. The underlying of the backstrap was processed and dried to create a sinew (a tendon attaching muscle to bone) material cut into strips to use for a strong and lasting binding and sewing material—a rope or string of sorts. Deer tails adorned headdresses and other bodily dressings for fashion. The metacarpals, or finger/toe bones, were worked to create a serrated edge, and these were used as scrapers.

Not only were deer bones a quality material from which to create tools, the larger bones also held tasty marrow used for cooking and eating. Not being people who would waste anything that was considered a gift from their creator, bone marrow was extracted from deer bones regularly. Archaeologist Stephen House of east-central Ohio has unearthed numerous bones to support the idea. "When looking over a deer bone, you can tell if it has been cooked in or over an open fire or boiled in a pot," said House. "The Indians boiled many bones to retrieve the marrow as it was a bonus addition to their diet." The then hollowed bones were sometimes used as a small quiver to hold arrows. "The Indians valued the deer highly, and the bones of those deer are commonly found throughout the state in remnants of Indian villages and additional sites in between. Deer bones were also split to make hair dress items for women's hair."

Hooves were hollowed out and dried to be added with others to make a rattle used during ceremonial dances and other celebrations. Rib bones made scrapers for hide work and arrow and bow maintenance or for building. The deer's stomach lining was dried and shaped into water toting containers or for other packing uses. The Indians who inhabited the region that is now Ohio were also fine fishermen. Using spears and arrows as fishing gear was common, but fishing hooks cut from deer bones were competent as well. Antler tips were cut from the antler body, and the center was bored out to compose an arrowhead. Even though most arrowheads were knapped from flint (using a portion of an antler to shape the arrowhead's edges), antler-tip arrowheads were not uncommon. "At one southern Ohio site, we discovered an antler point arrowhead with a broken tip," said House. "The break was done after the arrowhead was made, and it's very likely the missing tip is imbedded in a deer bone remaining on the site. A bone of a deer killed with an antler tip arrowhead."

During the 1500s, the deer was still a valuable resource throughout the state. Although the Indians were more focused on the multiple uses of the deer for sustaining the tribe, it was still honored in ceremonial ways. Headdresses and other human body adornments were decorated and enhanced with deer antlers and skins. Those same outfits were also used in deer hunting situations as a means to camouflage the hunter and his or her weapon to get close to place a quick killing shot. The taking of a wild animal was considered an honorable opportunity, not just merely a means to put meat over the fire.

An Indian village site in southeastern Ohio was situated in a fertile meadow along the Muskingum River during the late 1500s to the early 1600s; the importance of the whitetail was well represented here in the evidence left behind for archaeologists to survey. The village revealed several stages of the times the Indians lived through and how they adapted to the changes,

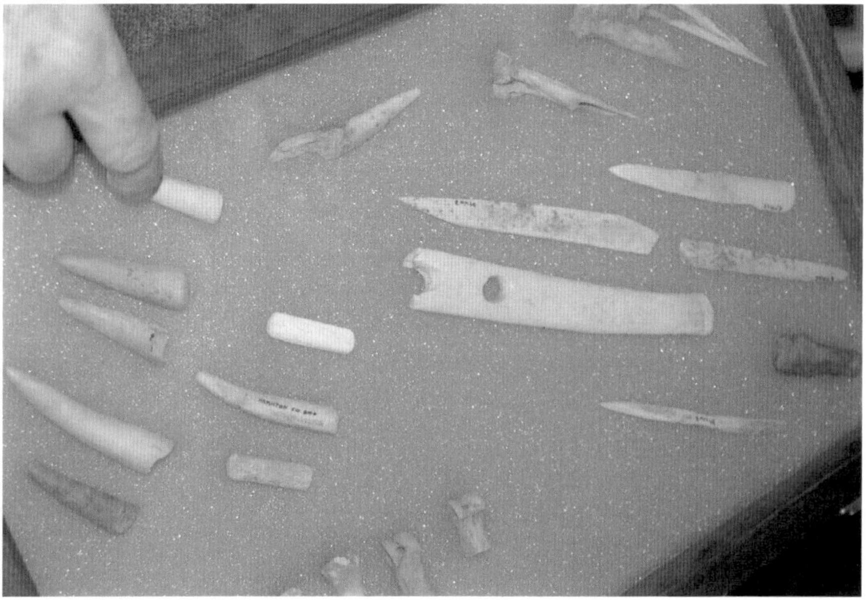

Antler tips were used as arrowheads and for ceremonial items such as rattles and dress enhancements. This collection is displayed by archaeologist Stephen House. *Robert Loewendick.*

such as the arrival of Europeans into the territory and the fluctuation of the value of the deer. The Indians built barricades around the village by inserting posts around the village's perimeter for protection against hostile intruders or attackers. Additional structures built inside the village, also made with posts, appeared a century later. These short (in length) interior walls were used as drying walls for deer hide. The hide drying walls were accompanied by smoking pits for hides. The hides were tanned by drying and being worked aggressively by diligent hands and working tools made of wood and deer bones. The drying process was performed by burning dried corn husks, which created much smoke that then enveloped the freshly scraped hide hanging on the post wall.

The described deer processing operation was common across the region, and as the English began to enter these lands from the east, in search for valuable deerskins, the Indians realized the deer's commercial value. The 1700s saw the transition of deer becoming an even more valuable trade item than before. The colorful beads and copper articles were favored by the Indians, and deerskins were their best tradable to gain the treasured decorations from the newcomers. The English were forbidden to cross the Appalachian Mountains; this rule was proclaimed by the English king. But after the deer were hunted extensively and the deer population was decimated on the east side of the Appalachians, the English followed the lure of many whitetails inhabiting the western side. The French and the English tried to outdo the other in trading with the Indians. Loyalty to one or the other changed often, as both sides caused trouble for the natives. What did remain was a sizable deer herd, and the value of a deer's hide remained high as well.

The pathway to the Ohio region was getting busy because of more trading opportunities with the French and English. Once again the primary trade items were products created from the white-tailed deer. But as the Indians traded away deer products, the people they were trading with were pouring newer, better tools into the Indian culture. With the advancement of tools also came the advancement of agriculture. These new skills supported with new tools were the beginning of the transition period for Indians in the Ohio Valley. In 1764, a released trader on his way to Pennsylvania was documented as to having 1,500 pounds of beaver pelts, 2,800 raccoon pelts and 2,000 pounds of deerskins with hair. In 1779, commonly traded items were already changing. Instead of beads and copper items, the traders were offering the Indians coats, assorted shirts of calico, plain white and checkered, rifles, gunpowder and lead.

The reverence for the deer that began in the 1300s was beginning to wane going into the 1800s for the Indians. During those five hundred years, the deer was 70 percent of the Indian's diet. When the French and English traders brought the commercial opportunities for the Indians to utilize the available deer herds, it would never be the same. Steel tools became the choice over deer-provided tools. "Though the Indians were being introduced to steel tools and were using them a great deal, the Indians remained resourceful," said House. "I've discovered a steel hoe that had arrowhead shapes cut from its edges. It was from the approximate year of 1815." The deer's value to the Indians, other than for hide trading, had dropped sharply. But the Indians improved the habitat for the white-tailed deer. With the clearing of land for expanding agricultural uses, many miles of wood edge were created. The deer populations began to swing upward as less hunting and more habitats became available. Then the white settlers began to infiltrate the Indian's lands. The deer herd of the Ohio region was about to be changed once again.

THE SETTLERS CAME, THE DEER WENT

It's amazing how deer went from being a sustaining resource to an economic monster.

—Stephen House, Ohio archaeologist.

The Ohio Valley was seeing a trickle of new people arriving, which soon turned into a flood. The settlers were putting down new roots as fast as the dust settled from their arrival. The new territory for these people offered fertile soils for super-productive agricultural practices. The problems standing between them and the farming opportunities they hoped for were stands of trees. Huge stands of forests connected to one another, with small meadows in between. With horses and mules, axes and saws, the forests were felled, tree by tree. In only a couple of decades, the land was looking like a foreign country. Though the farming industry was on the rise, the land that sustained a heavy deer herd for centuries could no longer do so.

By 1820, Ohio lands were primarily agricultural. As the settlers' fields expanded, the remaining deer and other wildlife began to take advantage of the new food sources. This caused the settlers to take aim at removing these living threats to their crops. A perfect example of the extent of the efforts by the settlers to stop the wildlife damage to their crops is the Hinckley Hunt. On Christmas Eve 1818, more than five hundred men organized and performed a wildlife-clearing hunt to remove damaging wildlife from their Medina County village of Hinckley. Working from the county's borders to the center, a surprising number of wildlife was killed: twenty-one bears, seventeen wolves, numerous small animals and three hundred deer.

Farther in the western portion of the state, the construction of the Miami-Erie Canal system was underway in 1825. The improvement of existing (and the creation of new) methods of transportation brought more people and land use to Ohio. In 1849, Ohio raised more corn than any other state. The remaining deer herd sprinkled across Ohio continued to take advantage of the abundant food source, but the farmers also continued their objective to rid the land of the deer, although the poorest of the settlers who did not farm or farmed very little utilized the deer to feed their families. Ohio's remaining deer still had a sustaining value. As the river traffic increased, businesses opened and flourished and more people came. Hunting seasons existed in the mid-1800s but were sporadic and never managed well enough to have a positive impact on maintaining a healthy deer herd. During the Civil War (1861–65), Ohio's population was busy surviving a war and keeping families intact. Deer were not a priority, except for the occasional meal to replenish exhausted soldiers at the many encampments.

By 1890, Ohio's industrial age was well underway. Factories and mines to supply fuel for the factories were changing Ohio's landscape once again. The natural resources during that time were not a priority of the state. Serious conservation efforts by individuals and the United States government would not be forthcoming for another forty years. The wave of people and their effects on the land slowly wiped the white-tailed deer from the Ohio region. By 1904, Ohio was without whitetails.

Chapter 2

THE TIMELINE OF THE DEER'S RETURN TO OHIO

The 1920s and 1930s: Deer Delivered

Conservational practices were being tested across the state with and for several natural resource subjects, the white-tailed deer being one of them. The interest in having deer hunting back in the state steadily grew through the two previous decades, beginning soon after the deer were extirpated in 1904. As with most negative impacts on natural resources of those times, the deer weren't as appreciated until they were gone. In 1922, with guidance and labor from the Division of Conservation and volunteers, deer were trapped in neighboring states and released in southern Ohio's Scioto County. The State of Ohio had purchased nine thousand acres of rugged forestland capable of harboring a deer herd. The land was named after one of America's greatest conservationists, Theodore Roosevelt. At five dollars per acre, the Theodore Roosevelt Game Preserve was bought. Securing this land was not only a winning situation for wildlife but also for those wanting to hunt deer once again in Ohio.

Additional land tracts were added following the initial purchase. The acres were compiled, as were the efforts of conservationists to bring the white-tailed deer back to Ohio. The newly acquired wildlife preserve came with a catch regarding hunting: the administration would not allow hunting on preserve grounds until 1933, not even then for deer but rather for small game only. This was so that wildlife could rebound to sizable populations

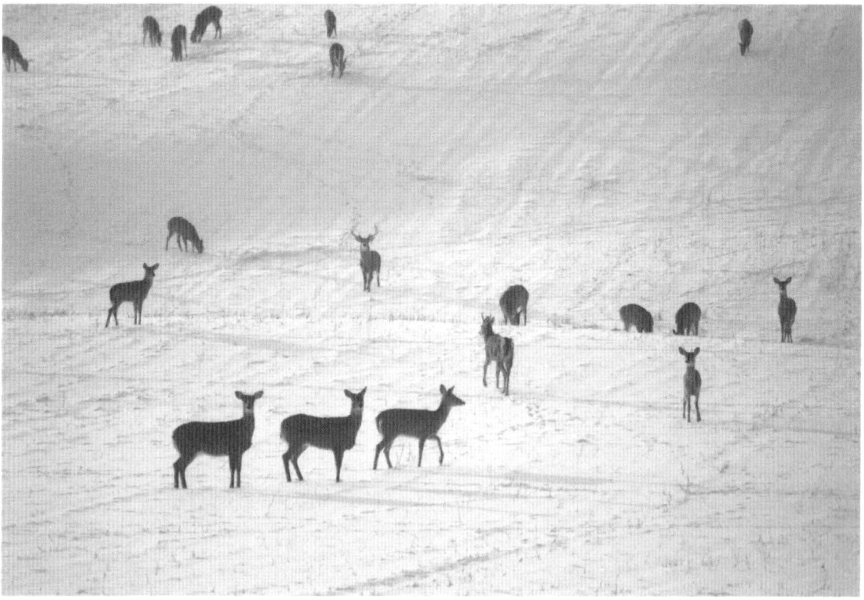

Winter deer herds bring the whitetail community together in search of food. Late-season hunts normally put hunters in not-so-pleasant hunting conditions. *Robert Loewendick.*

similar to the ones existing before overhunting and land clearing took their toll during the previous century. Starting soon after the Roosevelt Game Preserve was bought, the efforts to trap and deliver deer to the preserve were increased. Deer were purchased and caught, starting with two hundred deer that were released in a controlled, eight-hundred-acre corral. During the next decade, the small herd grew to about one thousand deer. Ages and sexes of the deer were not well documented, but the reestablished deer herd was healthy.

In 1932, the deer that remained in the hold (numerous deer had escaped to the expanse of the preserve) were released. Other than an outbreak of a bacterial infection the following year, which killed approximately 25 percent of the herd, the deer blended into the preserve well. In 1935, the Roosevelt Game Preserve was dedicated, along with three others in the state, as Ohio's first wildlife areas. The labor and planning to bring back wildlife and hunting was having some success. The land was there and the wildlife, too, but even then a wildlife and land management plan had to be established. During the rougher and rowdy days of the 1930s, one concern that the preserve managers had was policing the anxious hunters (or, more so, poachers) from devastating the growing deer herd. Additional game protectors were hired and assigned to the Roosevelt Game Preserve to assist and protect the deer's return to Ohio. The core of Ohio's deer herd existing today came from the restocking and release into the Roosevelt Game Preserve.

Scioto County was not the only Ohio site where deer numbers were on the rise. Southeastern and northeastern Ohio borders were seeing natural migration from neighboring states. Deer were reported in twenty-eight counties in 1937. As the deer made their way around the new wildlife preserves and into the other edges of the state, the call for hunting seasons began to get louder. The thoughts of the early game managers were focused on allowing the deer herd to grow to an agreeable size for all Ohioans—not only for the hunting crowd. As the 1930s came to an end, the farmers in the northeastern edge of Ohio were beginning to deal with crop damage by whitetails. The herd was growing and spreading slightly, which created the need for additional game management plans on a wider scale.

A person who may have had the biggest impact on Ohio's early deer management planning and had a clear vision for Ohio's deer and deer hunting future was Floyd Chapman, a wildlife research specialist. He foresaw the possibility of Ohio's white-tailed deer becoming the most sought-after game animal that it is today, for both the hunting aspects and the economic impact for the state. Many of the effects of Chapman's deer management research and decisions are still referred to today by modern wildlife biologists.

The 1940s: Season Opens

In 1943, game managers offered a regulated hunting season to control the increasing deer population. This news traveled quickly, and would-be hunters began planning the journey to Adams, Pike and Scioto Counties. Ohio once again had not only deer but also a deer hunting season. The herd was not out of control, but the rising population numbers had the manager's attention. Early biologists reviewed other midwestern states and studied their management successes and failures. Ohio's game managers took their research and applied it to their deer herd. Time would tell if the opening of a deer season in 1943 was too soon or not. The first challenge was getting through the first hunt without too many troubles, for both the deer and the deer hunter.

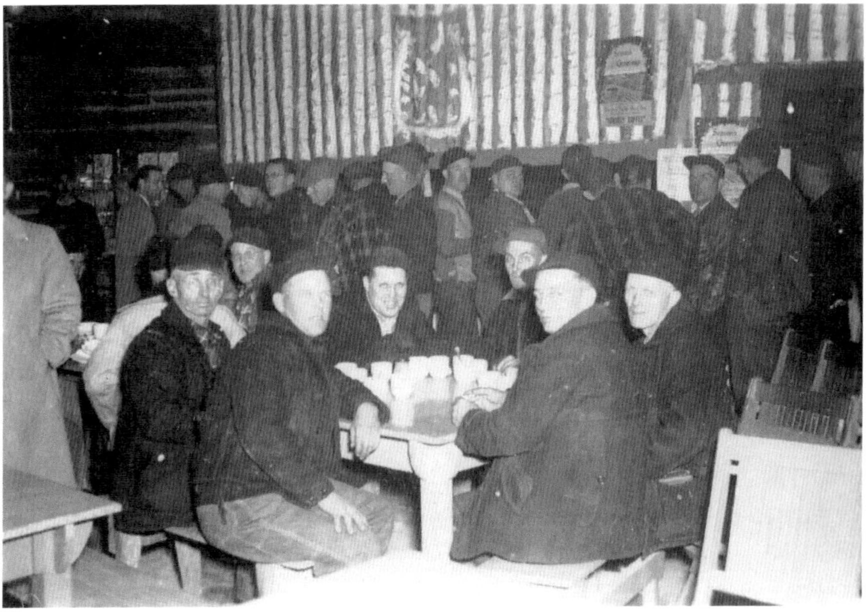

Men discuss the upcoming 1943 deer hunt in southern Ohio and wait for a chance to purchase a deer hunting tag to participate. *Ohio Department of Natural Resources.*

Hunters of various ages (including women) swamped the region in search of lodging and other needs to support them during Ohio's first modern deer season. Game managers considered their options and decided that a "first come, first serve" method would work best and would limit the number of hunters on the preserve. The buzzing crowd of 1,500 lined up at the Camp Oyo lodge (constructed by the Civilian Conservation Corps) at the Roosevelt Game Preserve, now Shawnee State Forest. That specific location only had 800 permits, and another preserve station had 200. The number of hunters allowed to hunt inside the preserve was limited for safety reasons. No hunting accidents were reported throughout the season. A few skirmishes broke out among the crowded line, but the attending law enforcement officials diffused the uproars. Hunting stories were shared between the waiting hunters, many of which took place in surrounding states. Questions were also swirling up and down the line regarding area deer sightings, what areas of the preserve held the best deer habitat and, if hunting on private land instead of the preserve, what amount of deer evidence existed there?

The 8,500 permits for the state's first deer hunt in more than fifty years were the tickets to adventure that hunters had been begging for years prior.

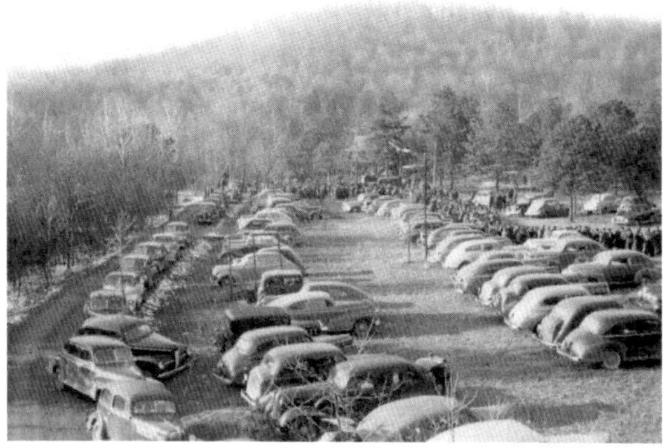

Cars and men lined up to have an opportunity to hunt Ohio's reestablished deer herd. *Ohio Department of Natural Resources.*

Even with the large number of hunters beating the bushes and roaming the hills and hollows with gun in hand, only 168 deer were killed in the buck-only twelve-day season. Hunters bagging a buck were required to mail their "kill card" to the Division of Conservation. The lucky hunters were popular individuals as they sat around campfires and tabletops retelling their stories. Conversations were also many as hunters, both successful and not successful, approached landowners in the region with hopes to gain permission to hunt deer on their property. Many did grant permission and even offered room and board in some instances. The three-county span had become a hot spot for hunters from near and far.

The 1944 deer season was also restricted to three counties that participated during the year prior, but the season was shortened to six days. Game managers discovered that the deer herd had grown 134 percent since 1937 to this second year with an open season. Deer were plentiful in and out of the Roosevelt Game Preserve. Private landowners claimed to see multiple deer at one time and several times throughout the day. For the 1944 season, 9,200 permits were sold, and 117 were filled by hunters. After the two seasons' tallies and other managing factors, a third season was approved. The 1945 season sold 7,700 permits, and only 62 kill cards were filled out. Because the harvest rates were not as the managers expected, they went back to rechecking their previous research to confirm that they were on the right track. There was no deer hunting season in 1946. The intentions of the game managers remained as they were when the restocking and hunt planning had begun: to provide as much opportunity as possible and keep a population of deer that could sustain an annual harvest.

After taking a year off, Ohio opened deer season for 1947. This year, though, the hunting would not occur in the three southern counties as

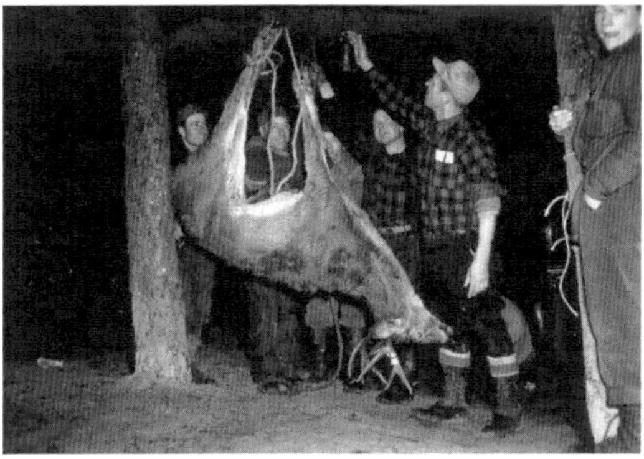

Several lucky hunters saw more than just deer tracks during the 1940s seasons. Successful deer hunters drew attention that lasted for days as the stories spread. *Ohio Department of Natural Resources.*

in '43 and '44. The '47 deer hunting season was opened up north in eight counties: Ashtabula, Carroll, Columbiana, Geauga, Jefferson, Lake, Portage and Trumbull. The reason for the opening of this season was not for recreational purposes, but rather for the management of crop-damaging whitetails. Deer crossing the Pennsylvania state line were finding sustaining habitats as they migrated, for whatever reason, to Ohio. Since this season was intended for a heavier reduction in population—to assist farmers who were already battling other elements, making farming a tough way to make a living—game managers adjusted the regulations. Although the season was gun-only and lasted for only three days, hunters could take either a buck or a doe. Being able to take a deer of either sex increased the odds of hunters seeing and having a shot at a deer. Permits sold totaled 9,669, and one thousand deer were killed.

The 1947 season was deemed a huge success, which pleased the game managers and the farmers. Game managers learned how quickly the kill rate can rise by adjusting one component of a hunting season, and farmers appreciated the fact that they now had a tool to keep crop damage to a minimum. The 1948 deer hunting season included five additional counties compared to last year's eight. As the amount of land available for hunting expanded, so did the interest in hunting deer. The Division of Conservation sold 23,044 permits. Approximately 1,600 deer were harvested in three days. There was no open deer season in 1949, as all of the locations harboring the white-tailed deer seemed to have their populations in check.

The 1950s: Deer Hunting Goes Statewide

In 1950, nineteen counties were the target of 23,044 permitted deer hunters. Of those, 3,500 took a deer. The exact number of kills during the '40s and '50s were not exactly accurate, as it was up to the hunter to report rather than appear at a checking station, and it was up to game managers to determine what the sex was of the deer killed and where it was hunted. No season happened in 1951, as game managers considered the previous seasons successful. The 1952 season was open to twenty-seven counties, with 14,081 permits sold, and 450 of those hunters took a buck as it was a buck-only season. With such a low harvest number during the geographically expanded season, game managers agreed to a consecutive season in 1953.

For the 1953 season, managers increased the counties involved to control the leading edge of the growing deer population and to increase the kill numbers in the counties that had been open the previous year. The hunting

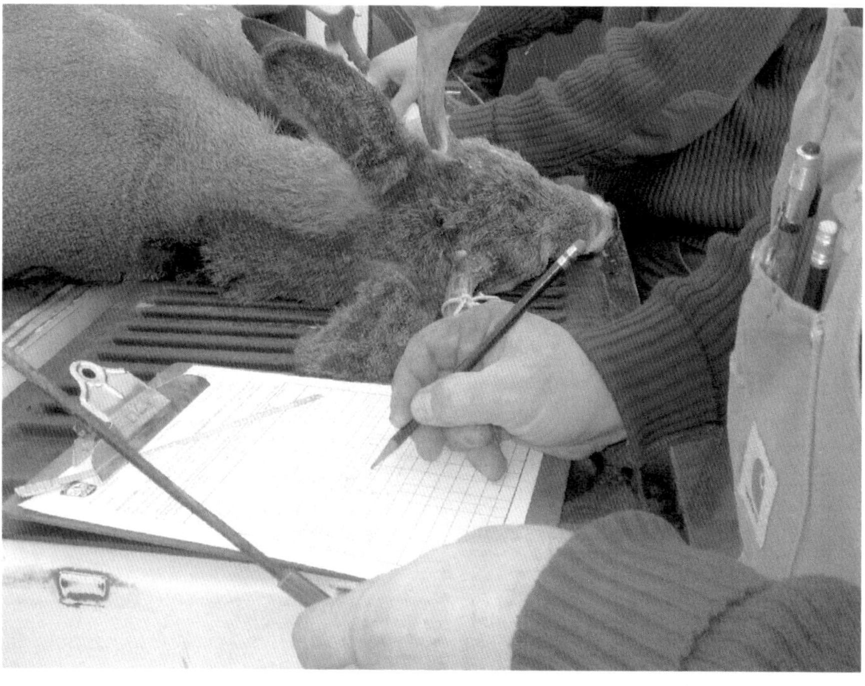

Ohio's deer managers continuously monitor and adjust conservation practices, including multiple deer hunting seasons, to keep the herd healthy. *Ohio Department of Natural Resources.*

force was successful—30,033 permits were sold and 4,000 were filled. As in the previous seasons since the modern era of deer hunting commenced in Ohio with the 1943 three-county season, it was the hunter's responsibility to report his success to the Division of Conservation.

The deer harvest totals of 1952 and 1953 determined that there would be no need for a deer season in 1954. The 1955 season was opened to forty-two counties, some of which were still seeing the leading edge of Ohio's deer population expansion—36,419 permits sold and 4,200 permits filled. The deer population was growing at a steady pace, and with strong demands from Ohio citizens (hunters, farmers and, now, urban landowners) to expand the deer season, the deer season of 1956 was open to all eighty-eight counties. Since the majority of the deer population was still concentrated in the southern and eastern portions of Ohio, deer permit sales did not sky rocket as expected. During the 1950s, most hunters from western Ohio traveled to the south and east to satisfy their hunger for recreational deer hunting. There were 48,263 permits sold and 3,911 filled.

From 1957 to 1960, all eighty-eight counties were open to an annual deer season. Deer hunting permit sales gradually dropped off (1957: 46,466; 1960: 27,430), and so did the deer harvest totals (1957: 4,784; 1960: 2,584). According to Ohio's current (2010) leading white-tailed deer biologist Dr. Mike Tonkovich, the 1950s was a decade of trial and error and of adapting deer management techniques learned from other states with Ohio's expanding (both in number and location) deer population. "My predecessors were focused on growing the deer herd and tuning hunting seasons to manage the growing herd," said Tonkovich. "During the fifties, it was all about the seasons, during the sixties, the focus was transitioning to the animal."

The 1960s: A Plan Comes Together

During the 1950s, wildlife managers focused on length of season; buck-only or antlerless condition; and what counties should be included. As the 1960s began, wildlife managers took a step back and reviewed each season since 1943 and where the deer stood and where they should go or not go. Although Ohio's deer herd was increasing, the fact was exposed that a highly successful deer hunting season could turn the deer population the other way. If a huntable population was to be maintained and not merely managed to reduce conflicts with humans but also used for sport, Ohio's deer management plan needed some work. In 1961, the statewide deer season was closed as wildlife biologists drafted a deer management plan that would suit the state and white-tailed deer enthusiasts of all kinds.

Also in 1961, a young wildlife biologist was hired to compose a long-term deer management plan. This Penn State grad, Charles Nixon, brought fresh deer management ideas to Ohio's planning table. After a couple years of experience, Nixon and assistants authored a document that would become Ohio's blueprint for the state's deer management plan going forward. The document was titled *The White-tailed Deer in Ohio: Its Past and a Look at its Future.* Deer season reopened in 1962 following the one-year break and was open statewide. Down from 1960, 23,049 permits were sold and 2,114 were filled.

The newly devised deer management plan was still in its infancy, but the plan's successful strategies would begin to materialize over the next few seasons. Several factors early on in 1962 were evidence that deer management

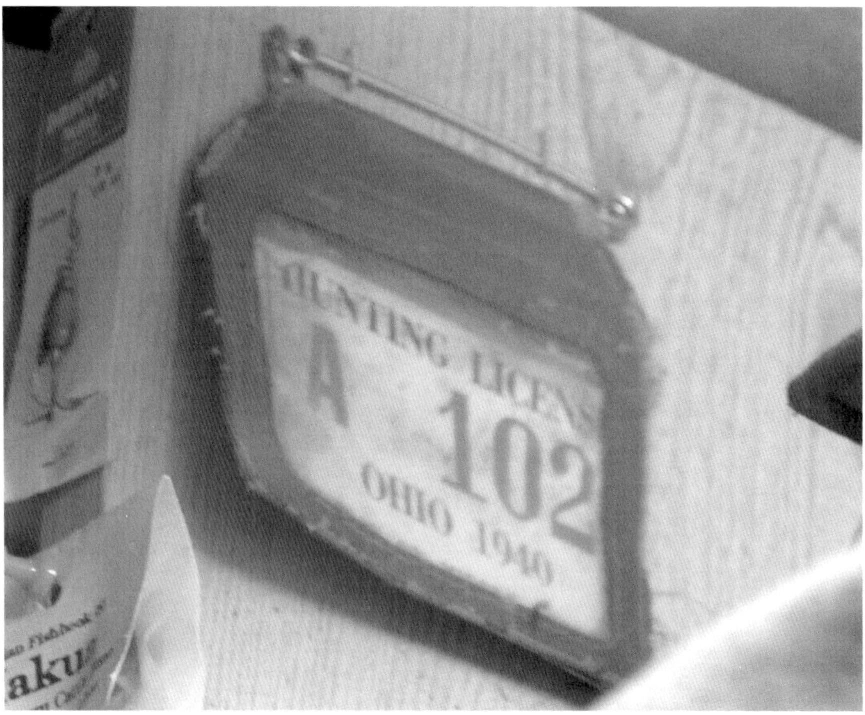

Hunting licenses that were once displayed proudly on hunter's hunting coats now hang on walls as a tribute to their respected hunting heritage. *Robert Loewendick.*

in Ohio was changing, such as mandatory registrations, field studies, population dynamics and food habit studies. Ohio's diverse geography amplified deer management challenges. The hill country of the south and east required different management practices and regulations compared to the plains lands of the western half of the state. Wildlife biologists decided to separate the states into zones for more accurate research practices and application of hunting regulations. The research led biologists deeper into what made the deer population tick. The database that wildlife biologists added to and drew from during the early '60s was instrumental for future Ohio wildlife biologists.

In 1965, statewide deer hunting was stopped, as only thirty-six counties were involved. Permit sales dropped dramatically (12,808, with only 406 deer taken) because of this and because international troubles held the attention of many Americans. As the 1966 deer season came into view, forty-eight counties were on the horizon. Permit sales were also up at 24,079, and 1,073 deer were killed. This deer season also yielded approximately $4.6 million, which was an indicator to Ohio commerce of the benefits that big game hunting could bring to a state. The newly set regulations were intended to increase the deer herd slowly but steadily, and the numbers were showing that the plan was off to a good start. Throughout the rest of the 1960s, permit sale numbers continued to increase gradually, as did the harvest totals. In 1968, Ohio held its first primitive hunt, for hunters who were also attracted to the hunting ways of the 1700s and 1800s. With the addition of primitive weapon season and archery season, hunters now had more options that satisfied the desire for big game hunting opportunities in Ohio for the most part. The 1969 season opened in fifty-six counties with 45,078 permits, and the season ended with a tally of 2,105 deer harvested. Compared to the 1957 season with nearly the same number of permits sold, the harvest total in 1969 was about half. With only fifty-six counties open instead of all eighty-eight, the wildlife biologists had a more accurate and successful control on the deer population.

The 1970s: Growing the Herd

Regarding the modern era of the white-tailed deer management of Ohio, the 1970s were fairly quiet. The management plan initiated in 1962 was working well, and the sales of deer hunting permits and deer harvest totals

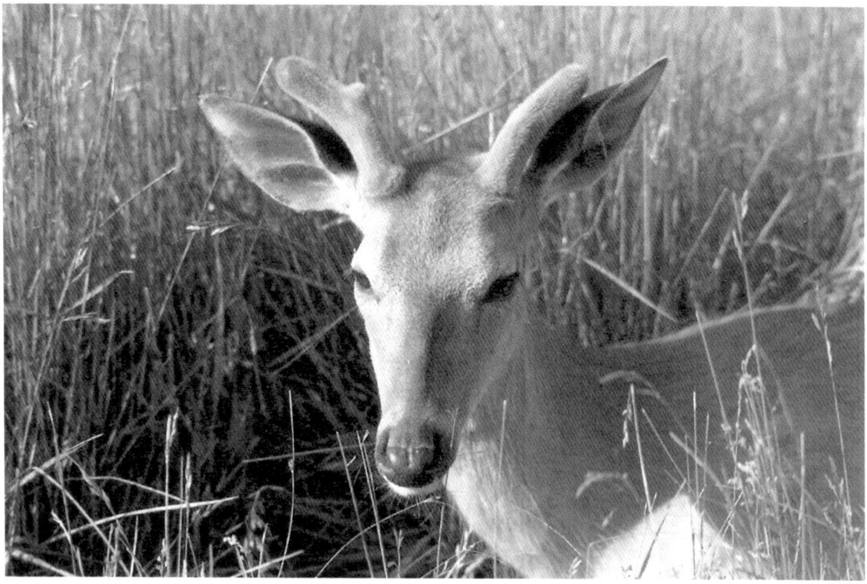

Proper nutrition for growing healthy deer and sizable antlers improved as agriculture practices progressed throughout Ohio. *Judy Wells.*

supported the plan's success. The deer population continued to grow across the state, but most of the deer population and hunting opportunities were happening in southern and southeast Ohio. The thousands of acres of state and national forestlands provided plenty of cover and food sources to sustain the herd. Both resident and nonresident hunters were taking advantage of the quality deer hunting awaiting them in the less people-populated counties.

In 1970, the deer season was open to fifty-one counties. Nearly 55,000 permits were sold, and only 2,387 deer were harvested. The following year, sixty-three counties were open, with 74,758 permits sold and 3,831 deer harvested. The numbers of open counties, permits sold and deer harvested were still on the incline. Wildlife managers opened counties to hunting only if the available deer population of that county could accommodate the reduction without endangering future hunting possibilities. The northeastern portion of Ohio was again experiencing crop damage by deer, and wildlife managers were beginning to hear more from the Ohio Farm Bureau about deer and farmer conflicts. Those counties were reviewed by wildlife managers with crop damage in mind first and hunting second. As a whole, though, the plan continued to focus on growing the deer herd across the state. In 1973, deer hunting permit sales went over the 100,000 mark at 107,933. The fifty-nine open counties had 7,594 deer taken.

The crossbow was legalized in 1976, which expanded hunting opportunities for hunters of many physical levels. Today, the crossbow is responsible for 20 percent of Ohio's total deer harvest. In 1979, every county was included in the deer season, with 193,764 permits sold and 34,874 deer harvested. The western and northwestern portions of the state were beginning to see a few deer roaming the edges of woodlots sprinkled about the wide-open fields. Ohio's deer herd was following the wildlife manager's plan, as were the hunters who returned each year to take advantage of Ohio's wildlife treasure.

THE 1980S: ENJOYING THE HARVEST

Ohio's deer herd was a sight to see, and hunt. The whitetail was becoming an asset for thousands of people involved directly or indirectly with Ohio's whitetails. Wildlife enthusiasts had a big game animal roaming their state not only for hunting but also for simply observing. For wildlife managers, this was a bonus for their management efforts—Ohioans with diverse outdoor pursuits were appreciative of the whitetail's presence. Managers dealt with the occasional trouble spots in which a deer population burst would create trouble for farmers by damaging crops. The 1980 deer season was the first year that permit sales rose above 200,000, with 216,055 and 40,499 deer harvested.

Something that was out of wildlife manager's control was another boom in population and expansion: people. A wildlife researcher with the Division of Wildlife, Robert Stoll Jr., studied the effects of deer living in heavily human-populated areas of the state with the blooming deer herd. As the hunting seasons continued to reduce the herd, wildlife managers offered antlerless deer permits to the more deer-populated counties via a lottery system to increase kill numbers in the southeastern region. This was a popular addition that led to more interest in hunting Ohio's deer, since the odds of taking a deer was increased—that is, if the hunter was drawn from the many entries into the antlerless permit lottery. This worked fairly well, except that the managers were finding that some of the antlerless permits were not being filled. Additional management problems were experienced,

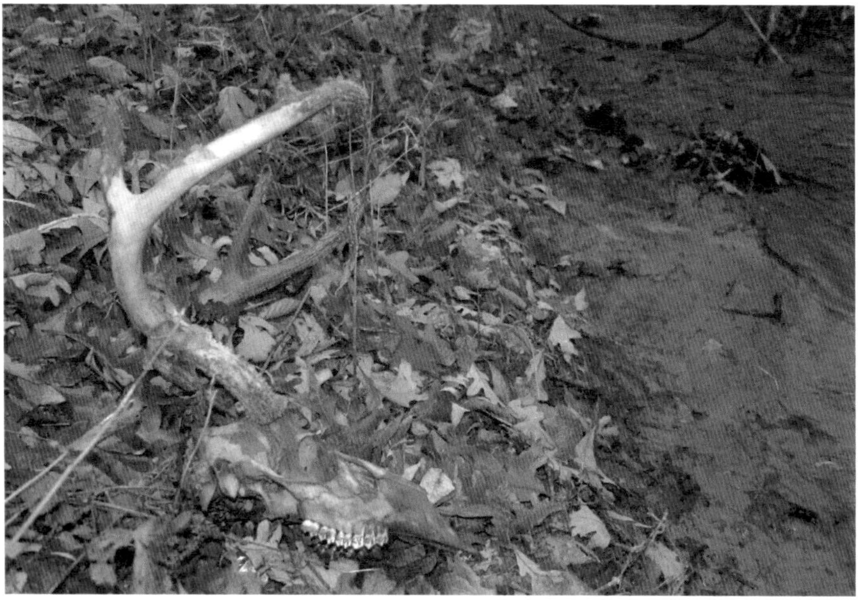

Ohio's deer herd has only been affected by disease a few times, which were limited to the eastern and southern portions of the state, and for a brief time. *Robert Loewendick.*

and in 1984 selected counties across the southeast were opened to hunting either sex. After a couple seasons of this, wildlife managers were pleased with the results and so were hunters. Research data compiled during the 1980s painted a picture that pleased the Division of Wildlife, as well. Ohio's deer herd remained strong and spreading, and hunting the deer was becoming more popular. In 1988, 373,435 permits were sold and 100,674 deer were harvested.

A new problem was beginning to develop across the eastern and southern regions. Hunters were not being welcomed on some private lands as in years prior. Although hunter access was being limited, abandoned farms and reclaimed coal mine lands were reverting to more favorable deer habitats. This factor, along with the hunters being denied access, allowed the deer population to grow more than expected. Wildlife managers continuously adjusted the hunting seasons to accommodate the herd.

THE 1990S: CHANGE OF PLANS

The deer population was still on the rise as the 1990s arrived. Wildlife managers had their hands full with growing complaints from farmers, the auto insurance industry and hunters who wanted more permits. The concerns were met with more adjustments to seasons and bag limits. In 1990, there were 98,468 deer killed statewide. In 1992, permit sales were 359,250 and 126,113 tags were filled. The rise in the deer population was not exactly what wildlife managers were expecting according to their field studies and methods of estimating numbers. Hunting results were only one element in the manager's deer population equation; deer/car crashes were another. The two showed nearly the same results for several years. As the deer population began to look a bit out of hand, wildlife managers realized that the deer hunting harvest numbers were not supported by the deer/car numbers. More cars were on the road now, which increased deer collisions. After wildlife managers adjusted their population tracking system, it was evident that the need existed to reduce the herd more heavily.

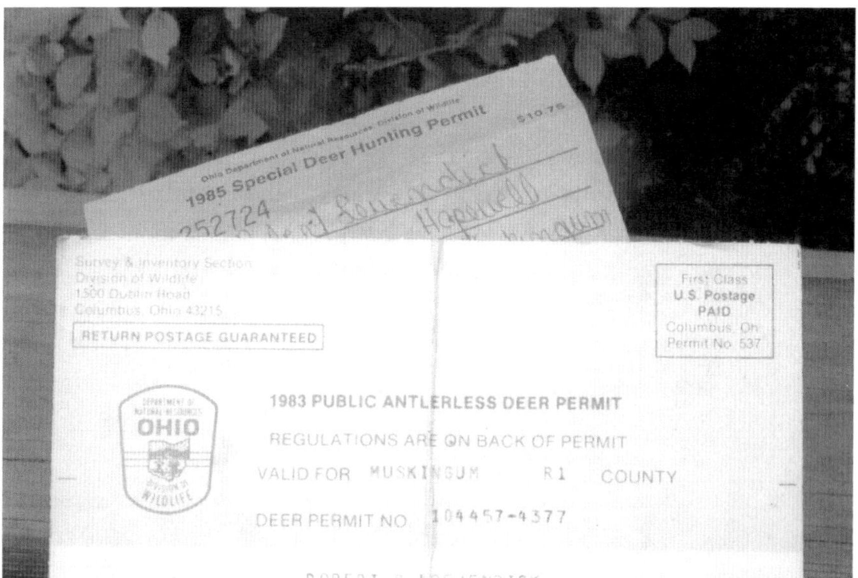

Antlerless permits were a bonus for hunters who applied for them in select counties in 1983. *Robert Loewendick.*

During the 1994 and 1995 seasons, the Division of Wildlife provided hunters with more opportunities to take more deer. The antlerless section of Ohio's deer herd was the prime target to reduce the herd to a more manageable number. According to Pat Ruble, the now retired executive administrator of Wildlife Management and Research with the Division of Wildlife, hunters responded to the offering. "Our research revealed the deer herd needed to be seriously reduced going into the mid nineties and so we accommodated that need by increasing hunting pressure," said Ruble. "We were successful in accomplishing that goal, as we reached record breaking harvests." The following couple years, hunters began to complain that the Division of Wildlife had allowed too many deer killed. In 1998, the deer population began to level off from the previous population reduction years started in 1995.

Although hunters were concerned about the deer population declining, there was success in reducing deer crop damage and auto/deer collisions. The deer population was at a sustainable level in the minds of wildlife managers, and so hunting regulations were adjusted once more. During the 1995 season, 496,890 permits were sold and 179,543 deer were brought to check stations. In 1999, 361,125 permits were sold and 126,770 deer were killed. Deer habitats were still sufficient around the state in general, and some areas became lairs that allowed bucks to accumulate years of living and grew to trophy size. As the next decade would prove, Ohio had become a deer hunting state in which hunters could not only easily fill their tag but also possibly bring home a trophy as well.

2000 to Present: Supreme Herd, Supreme Hunting

The dream deer herd was real in Ohio: lots of deer, many big bucks milling around in between and a wildlife management system that worked. Not only were Ohioans having the deer hunts of the century, hunters from outside Ohio's borders were as well. Nonresident deer hunting license sales were increasing each year, and during this decade, the sales would continue to rise. Towns in each county were reaping the economic benefits that deer hunting had brought to their region. Deer hunting in Ohio was (and is) a bargain of an adventure compared to deer hunting in midwestern states.

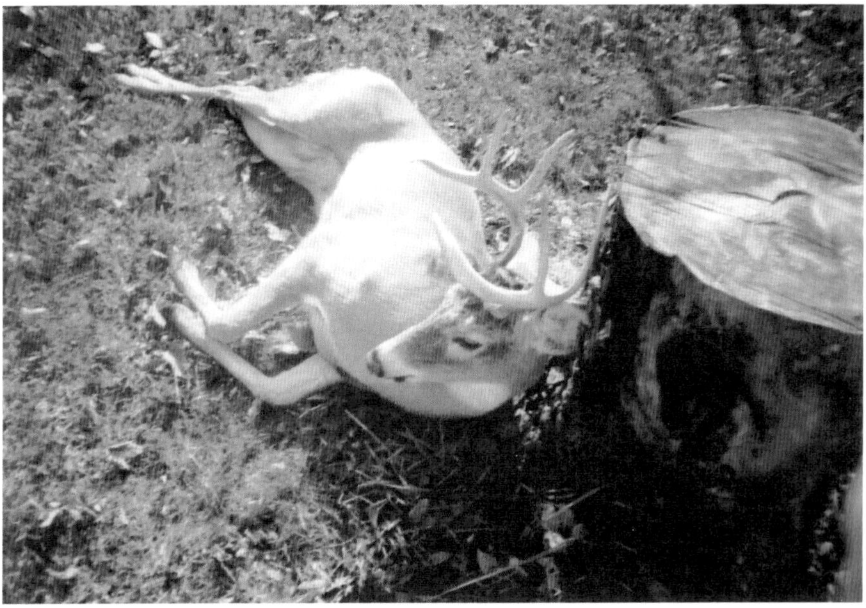

Strong, healthy deer such as this harvested buck is an example of successful deer management and an abundance of agriculture throughout Ohio. *Robert Loewendick.*

Still, Ohio's wildlife managers were focused primarily on the biological aspect of managing Ohio's deer, though social issues were just as important.

The 2002 season met 507,723 permitted hunters. The total harvest that year, including kills by license-exempt hunters, was 204,652. As the decade progressed, the need for more antlerless deer harvests became goal number one. The request by the Ohio Farm Bureau and others concerned and dealing with a deer herd of approximately 600,000 head in 2006 was understood and agreed on by wildlife managers. Antlerless deer hunting was entering a new level, as hunters focused on filling freezers as much as hunting for a trophy—so much so that several organizations, such as Farmers and Hunters Feeding the Hungry, were initiated to distribute donated venison to the less fortunate. In 2009, a record deer harvest was set once again, with 261,314 deer taken. The herd remains at an estimated 650,000 deer and were well established in every county in the state. More than 400,000 hunters of all ages, male and female, resident and nonresident, physically fit and physically challenged, are pursuing Ohio's white-tailed deer into the next decade. The solid deer management plan in place should provide first-class deer hunting in Ohio even further into the future. The folks who trapped and released the first deer into the Roosevelt Game Preserve would be proud.

Chapter 3
THE NORTHWEST

The northwestern plains of Ohio have seen deer hunters roaming the high grasslands, sneaking through woodlots and stalking the edges for elusive whitetails for centuries. When Ohio's deer herd was gone from the state by 1904, northwestern Ohio would be the last region in the state to see deer make a comeback. The majority of the northwestern's deer history occurred in the 1800s. The region's deer history is rich from those days, but with an established deer herd now, new stories are coming about each season.

The northern third of this region was once a swampy expanse, which made hunting deer there a tough physical challenge. During the early 1800s, the black swamplands were drained by settlers as part of land preparation for agriculture. Throughout the northwest, woodlots of one to several acres were homes to sizable, mature trees that provided an additional food source for deer. But much as it was across the state while the 1800s progressed, the landscape was changed and the results left deer little habitat, and so the deer would soon be gone.

Accounts of how many deer existed and what it was like to hunt them during those years were documented and published in a book and portions printed by a newspaper based in Archbold, *Farmland News*. The title of this collection of stories is *The Ohio Hunter*, compiled by James Nagel and Richard Helwig and published in 1866. The book told of the frontier life of Samuel E. Edwards in northwestern Ohio. With permission from *Farmland*

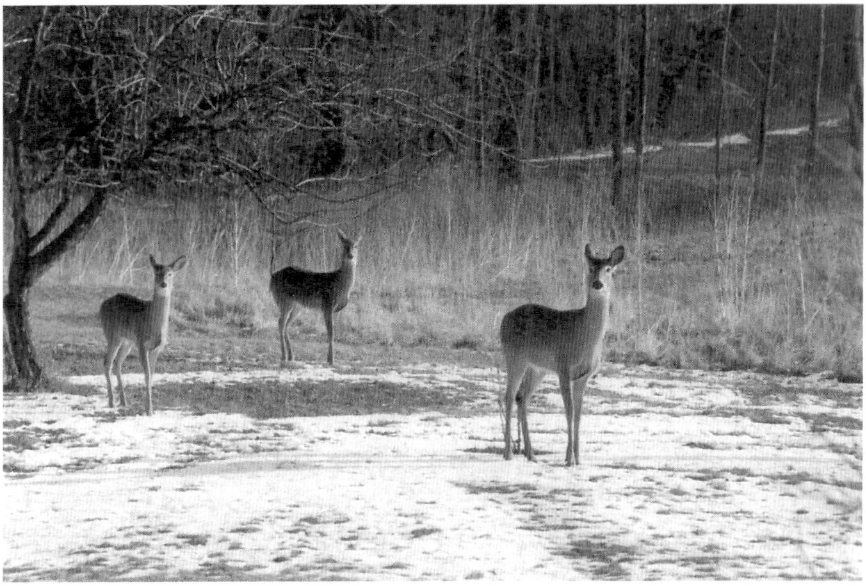

The plains of the northwest may not be prime deer habitat, but being interspersed with woodlots of various sizes has improved deer sustainment and the hunting with it. *Judy Wells.*

News, following is an excerpt that gives an insight of deer's importance to the northwestern Ohio settlers:

> *This was late winter and provisions were becoming extremely scarce. One morning at breakfast, my wife told me there was no more bread-stuff in the house and she guessed that now we should have to starve. I pointed to Old Killall, my rifle and told her that we would not starve while my old friend proved faithful. A few days previous to this, there had been a load of cornmeal sold in Findlay at two dollars per bushel. But as I had no money, I could purchase none and my gun and the immense forest were the only resource left me to feed myself and family. There was a nice snow on the ground and deer could be seen at a great distance. I took my wife's brother, a boy of 14, along with me and went hunting. We had proceeded several miles when we met a man hunting with neither dog nor gun. I asked him what he was hunting and he replied that he was hunting bees. He said that yesterday, the day being quite warm, the bees could be seen in great numbers and were even now lying thick upon the snow. I looked carefully about for some time and finally discovered the tree. I told my brother-in-law to cut*

> *down the tree while I returned home for buckets to carry the honey in. Using my compass, I started for home and had about four miles to go when a large deer started up in front of me. I took aim, fired and he was soon struggling his last. I cut his throat and left him lying there until I returned. When I reached home and told my wife what I had done, she looked at me rather incredulously for a moment. But seeing me arm myself with buckets for the honey, she concluded that I must be telling the truth and said, Well we shall not have to starve for a few more days. When I returned, my brother-in-law John had the tree nearly cut down and I soon finished it. We took out three buckets of pure honey, but did not have enough buckets for all of it and had to leave the rest for another time. Then we cut a long pole and, with some bark that we gathered, we tied the buckets at equal distances from each other along the pole. All things being arranged, John took one end of the pole and I took the other and we started for home. When we came to where the deer lay, we cut some bark and used it to hang the deer out of reach of the wolves. We were obliged to leave the deer there until morning because it was too late to return before darkness settled in. The next morning, we returned and secured the remainder of the honey and then went for the deer. When we reached it, the wolves wee howling madly round it but could not reach it. We frightened them off, cut down the deer and carried it home. My wife met us at the door and stated that we could live now, for we had meat and wild honey. There was more than 10 gallons of honey, most of which I took to Findlay and sold for 75 cents a gallon, using the money to buy cornmeal, coffee and tobacco. That was in January of 1834 and I went home feeling richer than I think several thousand dollars would make me feel now. I now thought it best to make some provisions for the coming year. I bought 10 acres and paid for it by cleaning 10 acres more. I built what we called a cabin-house and commenced clearing my 10 acres. When we wanted meat, I would take my gun and go into the woods and kill a deer or turkey or some other game with which the woods abounded.*

This story reveals not only how important a deer was to sustaining life by eating but also the positive effects gained mentally that were so important during tough times in the new lands. There were no grocery stores to run to, or money to spend, to get meat for the next night's dinner. The trusty rifle was the ticket to meat on the table—that and a steady aim. Deer were plentiful during the frontier days. Samuel E. Edwards killed thirty-eight deer during the fall and winter of 1834. For Edwards and other hunters, hunting deer with a single-shot, black powder muzzleloader like Old Killall often resulted in the hunter being forced to engage in hand-to-hand combat with a wily buck. Another common sight seen at homesteads at those times were multiple deer hanging at one time. Venison was a profitable, tradable good for families with good hunters and a steady source of meat for those families without skilled hunters.

Hunting year round was common practice for the hunting settlers. During the summer months and early autumn, deer spent much time near the rivers at night. Because of this, a new form of deer hunting came about: fire hunting. This hunting technique took advantage of the deer's need for a good water supply and the stillness of a canoe floating in the river's current. Large beeswax candles were placed in a blind in the bow of the canoe; the light mesmerized the deer, and the shadow from the blind hid the hunter. Hunters who mastered the method were able to float or paddle within a couple dozen feet from the staring whitetail. The technique was so successful that stories tell of hunters taking as many as eighty-five deer per year and sometimes up to six per night. Of course, that act is illegal today, but if your family's survival depended on the meat, as it did in the 1800s, putting deer on the meat pole was crucial. The same rivers that were the avenues hunters paddled to find game then still provide deer hunters good hunting opportunities along the riverbanks today.

Veteran outdoorsman Ralph Stout of West Unity was roaming the family farm in 1950s when he came upon a set of animal tracks in the mud. After the young boy looked the tracks over for several minutes, he was sure that the tracks were made by wild mountain goats. The Stouts were owners of several goats and other livestock, which assisted in young Ralph's reading of the track. After returning home, he told his father about his find. His father then informed his son that the tracks were not of wild mountain goats but rather those left behind by a white-tailed deer. He went on to tell Ralph about the efforts to reestablish deer in Ohio. Ralph couldn't remember if his father knew exactly how deer were being returned to their area, but the tracks were proof that a deer had walked there.

The watersheds that lead to Lake Erie harbor a fair amount of deer habitat, and hunters of the region favor them. The patchworks of agricultural fields that decorate the majority of the northwest complement the rivers that cut through them. The brushy edges of river runs and field lines are targeted for holding numbers of whitetails. For the last three decades, driving techniques

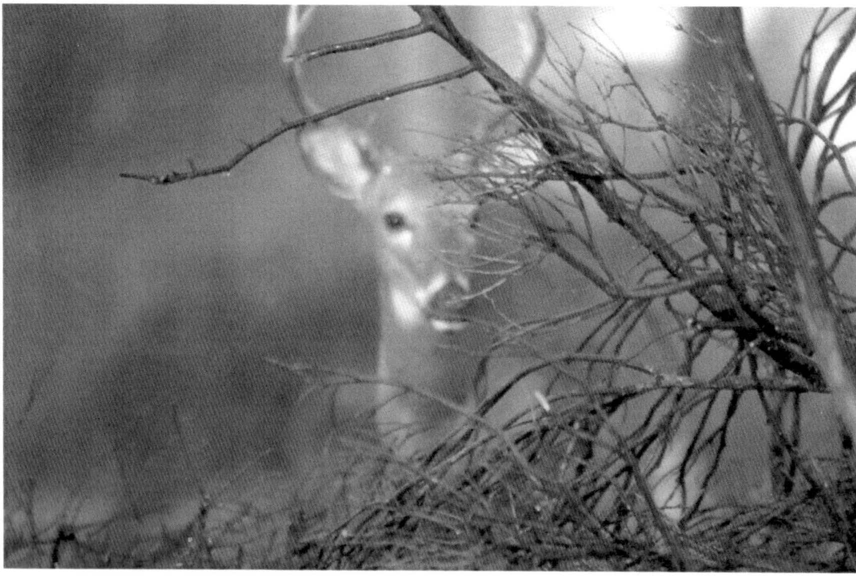

Deer began reappearing in northwest Ohio decades after they did in the southern region of the state. *Judy Wells.*

(or pushing) were, and are, highly successful methods for taking deer from the sporadic, smaller, wooded acres. Commonly, hunters would gather at a meeting point and then devise a plan according to the weather, time of day and number of drivers and standers. If the deer were expected to hold tight to their positions, then hunters would attempt to entice more hunters to join the drive to increase their odds of moving deer. Deciding where to focus hunts was not a difficult task, as the likely hiding spots were obvious even to the novice deer hunter.

Outdoor writer John Bennett of Lima was a kid during the 1950s and 1960s. It was rare for someone to kill a deer, let alone even see one. During those years, Bennett saw only about two dozen deer while spending countless hours in the field. Modern-day deer hunting of any measure didn't arrive in the northwestern quarter of Ohio until 1979. Deer harvests were few, but when they happened, the deer and the deer hunter were the topic of conversation for days afterward. According to Bennett, the good days of deer hunting became more serious in 1984. Successful deer hunting in the northwest continued into the mid-'90s. Now it's not a surprise if someone tells of seeing dozens of deer grouped at field edges.

Chapter 4

THE NORTHEAST

The northeast region's geography is quite diverse—from farmlands to metro areas, and from the Lake Erie shoreline to various lakes surrounded by open areas and woodlands. White-tailed deer of the northeast have survived well throughout their many habitat options. Cleveland, Akron and Canton subtract available lands for deer to roam, but plenty of miles of deer country still exist. Highways and byways intersect this region in all directions and through varied landscapes. Interstates provide today's hunters with ample and rapid access to productive hunting properties. The upper portion of the northeastern region is primarily flat but still has plenty of deer, and the hunters there have been successful in hunting the sporadic agricultural lands and adjoining woodlots. The southern portion of the northeast quad is made of hills and valleys. The deer that made the migration into Ohio from Pennsylvania found that this hill country not only provided ample food sources but also was a tougher landscape for living undercover. An advantage the hunters had for hunting this region was the watershed system left behind by coursing glacial melt waters. The waterways cut deep into some areas, which made for tough hunting, and just enough in others to create a milder challenging turf for hunters.

The northeast quarter of Ohio is the largest of the four researched sections of this book. After interviewing several biologists, hunters and landowners who work, recreate and live across these diverse counties, it was tough to get a simple summary of what hunting deer was like and is like there. Beginning in the northwestern portion of the northeast quad, the deer hunting was similar to the western region of Ohio. Flatlands with intermixed swamplands held very little deer. The same response heard from elder residents across Ohio's north and west was repeated up there: "If we seen a deer track, it was big news back then."

Going south from the northern portion, toward Columbus, the hills held more deer hunting stories. In the heart of Mohican Country is the Mohican Memorial State Forest. The Clear Fork and Mohican Rivers have created deer hunting routes for centuries, as all of Ohio's rivers have. This river and hills system is an Ohio feature, but similar landform combinations exist throughout the northeast but on a smaller scale. The northeast has been a preferred hunting region for decades. An abundance of historical stories from the 1700s does include deer and those who hunted them. Native Americans had several established Indian trails through the region, which was filled with wildlife to assist in sustaining the people. During the last seventy years, the increase in deer hunting pressure has continuously risen as the lands recovered from timbering and the extraction of Ohio's most abundant and valuable mineral: coal.

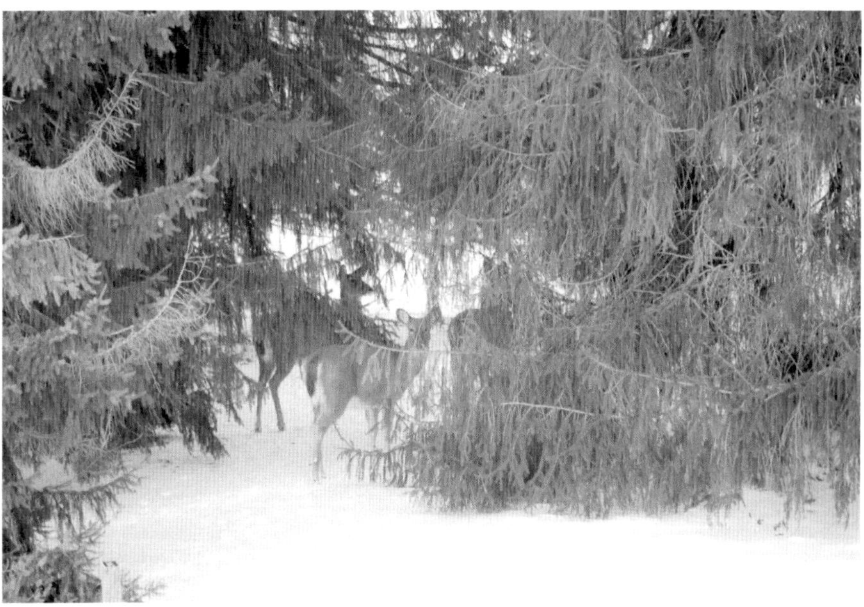

As a portion of northeast Ohio's agricultural lands reverted to forests and brushy habitat, the deer herd grew and so did the numbers of hunters visiting the region. *Robert Loewendick.*

In 1933, the Muskingum Watershed Conservancy District (MWCD) was created to construct, maintain and manage a flood control and water conservation program. Fourteen reservoirs would not only get a handle on flooding issues but also provide water for recreation. An additional bonus from the reservoirs, or from the surrounding lands, was the increase in sustaining deer habitat. Years after the dams and reservoirs became operational, the recreational values of the lands and waters were beginning to attract outdoorsmen. This included deer hunters soon after the season was opened for the first time in northeast Ohio in 1947. The Civilian Conservation Corps (CCC) implemented several programs around the northeast region and its woodlands and waterways during the late 1930s and early 1940s. Reforestation efforts by the CCC throughout the MWCD lands would create some of the best deer hunting opportunities the state had ever experienced.

One of the most frequently planted tree species was the crabapple tree. The trees worked well in the CCC's plan to reduce erosion and provide several species of wildlife a regenerating food source. According to Dan McMillen, a private lands biologist with the Ohio Department of Natural Resources, the crabapple tree was and is a staple in the northeast Ohio's deer herd. "In the '60s, it was regularly said you couldn't shoot a deer that didn't have crabapples in its stomach," said McMillen. McMillen also noted that northeast Ohio's diverse land supports different ecosystems, each one providing different food sources and sustainment challenges for deer and deer managers than the others. The CCC tree planting projects were extensive and successful. As the trees began to bear fruit for the deer to eat, the deer began to be seen across the region more regularly. Camping on the MWCD properties was popular with deer hunters through the 1940s and 1950s. Most of these deer campers were from parts of Ohio that were still not seeing any or very little deer. As for the deer hunters residing in the northeast, there were plenty of opportunities for taking a deer. The deer were as healthy as any deer in Ohio, or even more so than deer living in surrounding states.

Getting to the Deer

Deer hunting was often the discussion around northeastern Ohio wherever hunters gathered. The common complaint from deer hunters during the early seasons was that it was not legal to shoot does—bucks only. The deer herd was growing in northeast Ohio, and deer hunters wanted to take advantage of it. The farmers of the region agreed with the hunters, as the deer were a problem in the agricultural fields. Deer drives of various schemes were the most productive then, as hunters commonly hunted in groups. From the 1940s to the 1970s, it was common to see deer hunters moving across fields and through woods, pushing deer toward several standers waiting distances away. Sometimes the standers were only as far as the other side of the field or woodlot, or the standers might have had a mile or more in between them and the drivers. Most landowners owned hundreds of acres that could be hunted. Landowners were also much more likely to grant deer hunters permission to hunt their land, as many people knew one another around rural areas. Some

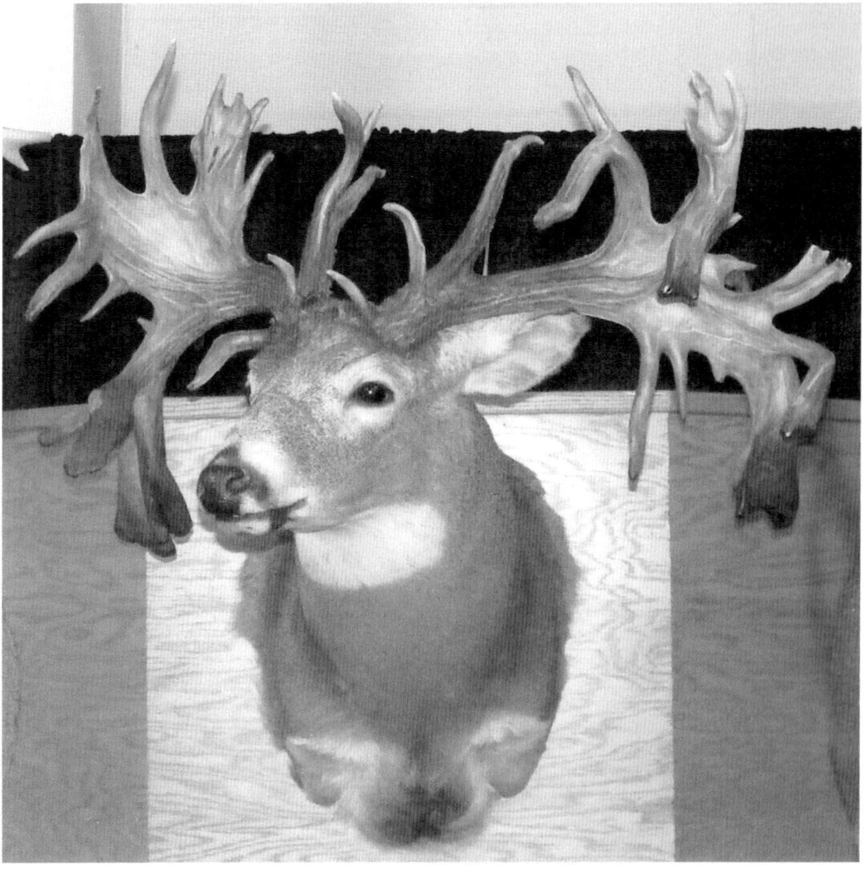

The infamous Hole-in-the-Horn buck was found dead along a railroad in northeast Ohio. *Ohio Department of Natural Resources.*

farmers would post an invitation for hunters to hunt deer on their properties to reduce or clear their fields of damaging deer. As the decades passed, farms were developed into residential lots. Because of this, the once wide-open lands that deer hunters were welcome to roam from farm to farm were now being broken up into small lots. These lots were no longer accessible for deer hunting, which created problems for the deer and the deer hunter.

For the Division of Wildlife, managing the northeast deer herd was a challenge because of the diversity in geography. What worked well in the extreme north didn't work so well near the central and eastern edges of the region. Licking County, a central Ohio county, was seeing deer move in from the north and east in about the 1950s. This was a sign that deer management practices were working regarding growing the deer herd. The blend of agricultural fields and the abundance of woodlands provided the perfect combination for growing the herd. As the herd expanded its range, it increased the population numbers in the already deer-populated regions such as the northeast. The northeast region began to attract more deer hunters as the news spread about the quality deer and the quality deer hunting that was to be had there. In previous years, before Ohio's deer herd became a serious hunting opportunity, deer hunters from Ohio would travel to Pennsylvania. Deer hunters were beginning to search out landowners in the northeast allowing deer hunting instead of traveling to Pennsylvania and other states.

As the northeast, or at least the eastern edge of that region, became more populated with deer and deer hunting opportunities, deer hunting traditions were beginning to form and prosper. Today, deer camps are common to accommodate nonresident hunters coming to take advantage of gun, archery and primitive weapon seasons. But during the decades before the 1980s, most deer hunters were local residents. It was common for a deer hunter to spend a day in the field with family, friends and/or neighbors in pursuit of Ohio's flourishing big game animal—and do so within a short drive from home, or even at home. Villages such as Deersville in Harrison County have seen their share of deer hunters, both local and nonresident, primarily because of location. Found on the map between two popular MWCD reservoirs, Tappan and Clendening Lakes, Deersville is, well, like its name, located in the heart of deer country. With hundreds of acres of public hunting access and plenty of deer habitats throughout those public hunting lands, deer hunters from across the state and across state lines continue to hunt deer there.

CHANGING LANDSCAPE

As the abandoned farmlands began to revert to wild vegetation growth through the 1990s, the deer hunting scene across the northeast continued to adapt. Record deer harvest numbers that were held primarily by southeastern counties were now being pushed by some in the northeast. Deer hunters responded by focusing on the northeast counties brining about the high kill numbers. Along with the plenty of deer to hunt, quality bucks sporting impressive antlers were also drawing attention. Deer hunting chatter across the state was still discussing the deer hunting results coming from the northeast. One element to more deer being harvested in the northeast was the involvement of the Amish community, which holds many dedicated white-tailed deer hunters. Even though the northeast region has numerous, highly human populated areas, the deer herd continues to thrive. During the 1990s, there were two winter kills of deer—one in Cuyahoga Valley near Akron and the second in Salt Fork State Park in Guernsey County. Neither event was any significant reason to be alarmed about the health of Ohio's deer herd statewide or in part. Each event involved low numbers of deer, and the specific local herds rebounded successfully.

Because of metropolitan areas being entered by a steady stream of whitetails, special archery hunts have been incorporated into deer management plans in the northern portion of the northeast quad. Special deer hunts are also held in specific situations, such as the ones at Salt Fork State Park, Camp Ravenna and Mosquito Creek. These hunts were not only necessary to control the resident deer herd, they also provide opportunity for young and physically challenged deer hunters. As the year 2000 came and passed, the northeast was experiencing another change to its deer hunting lands. About 98 percent of the land is privately owned. Most of the land today is off-limits to hunting for either safety or cultural reasons. However, some urban counties that used to give hunters the cold shoulder are now reconsidering because deer are frequenting lawns and flower plantings among expensive landscaping products.

Suburban sprawl has created tough deer hunting in many of the northeast areas. But human expansion has also created an abundance of hiding areas for bucks to grow big—deer hunters just can't get to them for the most part. Small woodlots and meadows near a housing development have become hot spots for dedicated trophy buck hunters to search out. More suburban

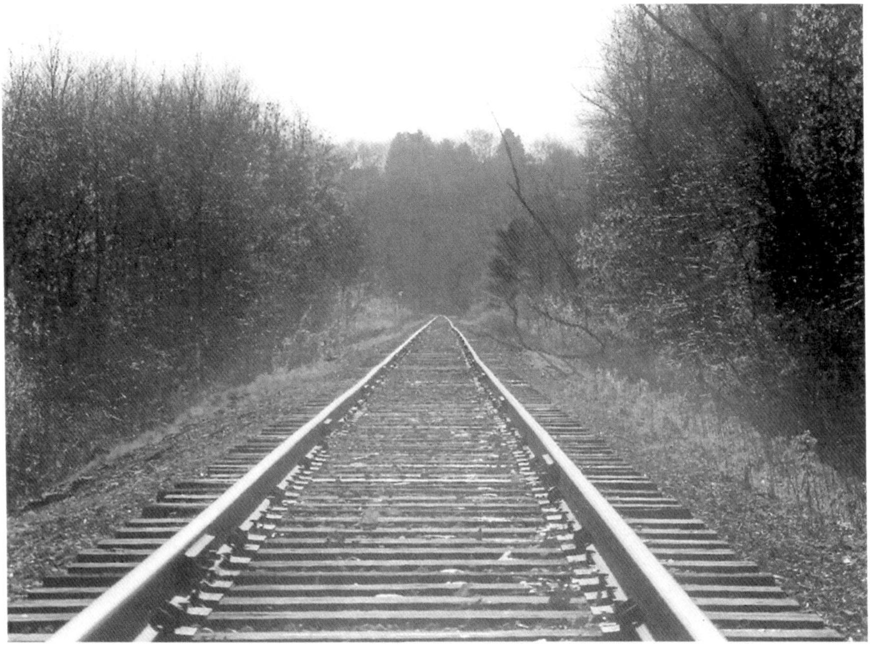

Railways and roadways provided access to prime deer hunting habitat. *Robert Loewendick.*

areas have also created more road frontage. The deer can be seen, but it is tough to gain permission to hunt them from landowners not accustomed to dealing with issues created by an overpopulation of a wildlife species. Leasing lands for hunting has become popular across Ohio and the nation, and the northeast Ohio is not exempt. For the average hunter, leasing a piece of land for recreational hunting is simply not feasible. But if several frugal deer hunters pool their funds, a quality piece of deer hunting territory can be had all to themselves.

Even though the northeast maintains an abundance of public hunting lands, land is being purchased (not leased) by individuals or groups to be utilized for wildlife enjoyment—for either hunting or simply observing. Wildlife enthusiasts are outbidding farmers for available land and then working the land to improve wildlife habitats to sustain current populations or to attract more. Seed sales for wildlife food plots have risen to surprising levels. Whether a food plot is being installed on a corner of a field edge or in woodland clearing of land already owned by a local resident, or whether it is intended to attract deer to a recently purchased acreage dedicated to hunting, the result of deer habitat improvement is the same. Wildlife managers claim that because land sales for hunting are on the rise, fewer local hunters are hunting on the northeast's many public hunting lands. However, more nonresident hunters are taking advantage of the quality deer hunting waiting on those public lands. Some of the best deer hunting in the northeast quad of Ohio is visible from or nearby two major highways.

Northeast Ohio was one of the first regions to see deer return to the state. From that time, thousands of deer hunters who walked the diverse hunting lands continued or initiated a remarkable deer hunting heritage. Old men shared stories with me about cruising the Ohio River bottomlands as boys, taking an occasional deer with a handed-down old shotgun. A proud mother told about her two boys tracking and killing a trophy buck in a deep hollow near Piedmont Lake—and then not being able to drag it out by themselves. A young hunter showed me antlers from a buck he shot with a bow in a cornfield north of Wooster—the corn was picked and the boy was standing in the open. A man from Canton, not a hunter, pulled a worn photo from his wallet, an image of his brother posing with a nice buck—his brother died in the Vietnam War. Northeast Ohio's deer hunting heritage is rich.

Chapter 5

THE SOUTHWEST

Ohio's southwest quarter has experienced the return of deer hunting to the state in the south, and it's also one of the last sections to see the herd's expansion going west and north. The extreme geographical transition from the west edge of the state southeast to the mini-mountains of the Shawnee State Forest is unique. The southwest region holds an abundance of deer hunting opportunities supported by the mix of rugged hills and hollows, prairie lands and scenic river bottoms, all in one corner of the state. The most southern counties along the Ohio River are rightfully nicknamed "the Little Smokies." Farther west and north, the landscape quickly flattens out into till plains with a patchwork of agricultural fields and several rivers, which created a few deep ravines and steep slopes able to support heavy timber. This wide range of geographical diversity has given deer and deer hunters an interesting playing field for survival and pursuit. Include remote ridge tops, lakeside meadows and woodlands along several state-managed lakes and reservoirs, miles of fence rows with skirting vegetation bordering wide fields, and it becomes obvious as to why southwest Ohio is the state's most diverse deer hunting region.

As detailed in an earlier chapter covering the whitetail's return to Ohio, Adams, Pike and Scioto Counties were the homes of the return of deer hunting in Ohio. The Roosevelt Game Preserve was created in those counties because of the mix of terrain and deer-sustaining habitats. The reintroduction of deer to the preserve was not only a success for the three

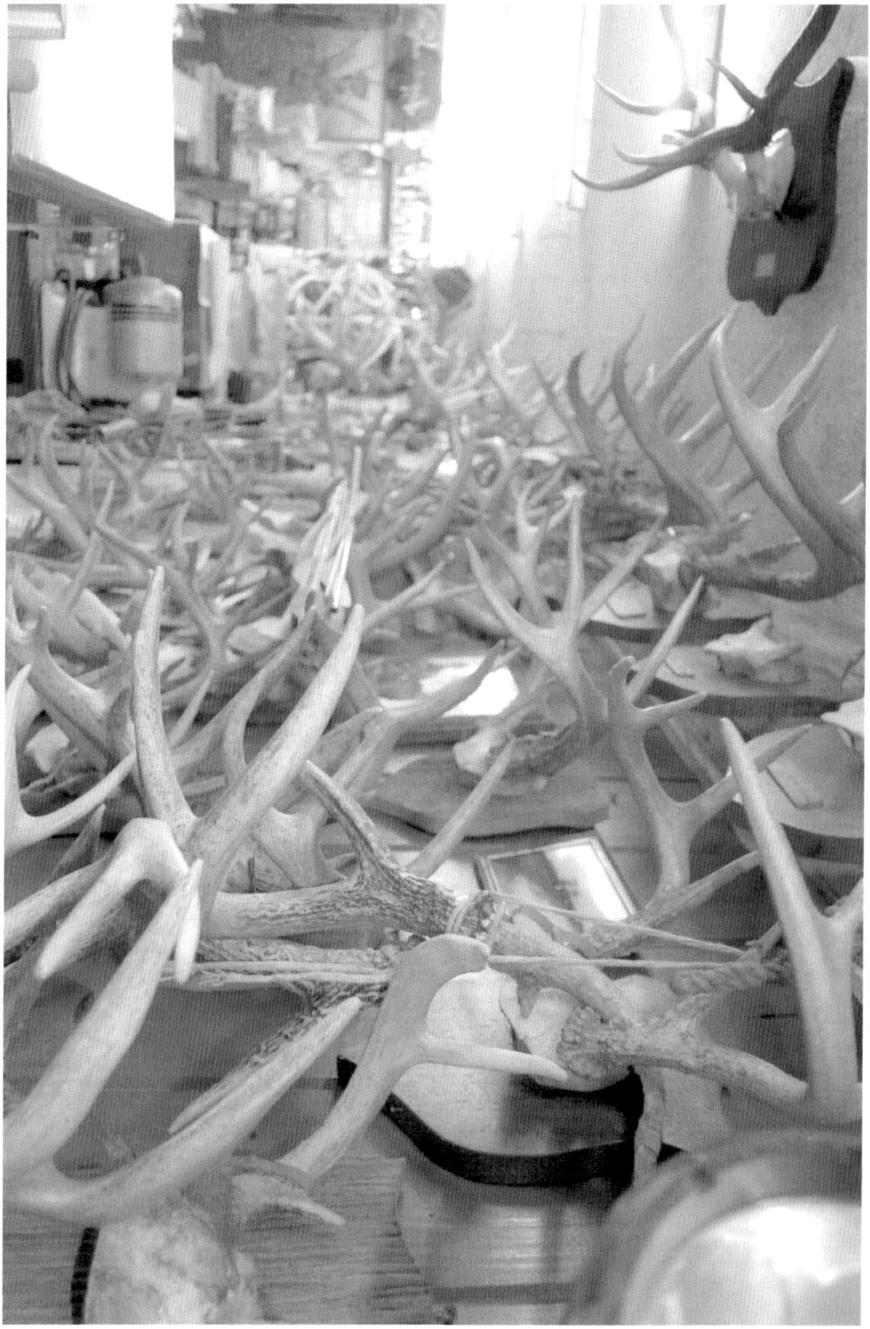

Keith Linkhart's collection of antlers and more compiled through decades of deer hunting in Ohio. *Robert Loewendick.*

counties but eventually for the entire state as well. Deer hunters from the western edge of Ohio now had a realistic deer hunting opportunity without traveling out of state to hunt. As the deer herd grew in numbers and their range spread, the counties surrounding the preserve began to see deer occasionally. Stories of sightings spread, and a few were supported by a deer body—some taken legally and some not so. The ones not taken legally were not for the antlers, as many poaching actions are intended today, but to put a supply of lean venison on the table for families living in tough economic times.

Ridge Runners

Adams County is considered by many to be the deer hunting hub of the southern portion of the Ohio's southwest. Deer hunting traditions run deep through the rugged hills and rolling mix of woodlands and fields in the descending foothills of the western edge of Appalachia. Adams County's grandfathers, fathers, sons and entire families are participants of some of the oldest veins of Ohio's hunting heritage. An avid hunter and outdoor writer from Adams County is Tom Cross. Tom has roamed the hills and valleys of Adams County for fifty years—many of which were in pursuit of whitetails. "Generations of our family are rooted in Adams County and its notable deer hunting heritage," said Cross. "We have seen the deer hunting go from good to great in this region. But the camaraderie shared by the hunters prevails over other aspects of deer hunting. Family and friends spending time together in this gorgeous country, interacting with the natural world, is special." Tom's introduction to deer hunting, like that of most southwest Ohio hunters, came at an early age. After conducting several interviews from the region, it was evident that a look at Tom's deer hunting experiences through the '60s and onward is an accurate representation of what deer hunting the southern portion of the southwest was and is about.

Raised in farm country with plenty of woodlands included, during the 1960s Tom was busy fishing the rivers and lakes of the region. As the white-tailed deer began to increase (although deer were nearly always present in Adams County) throughout the lands, as Tom's family owned neighboring acreages, the lure of the deer pulled Tom even closer to the woods. Bow hunting was a method of deer hunting established by the "modern" deer

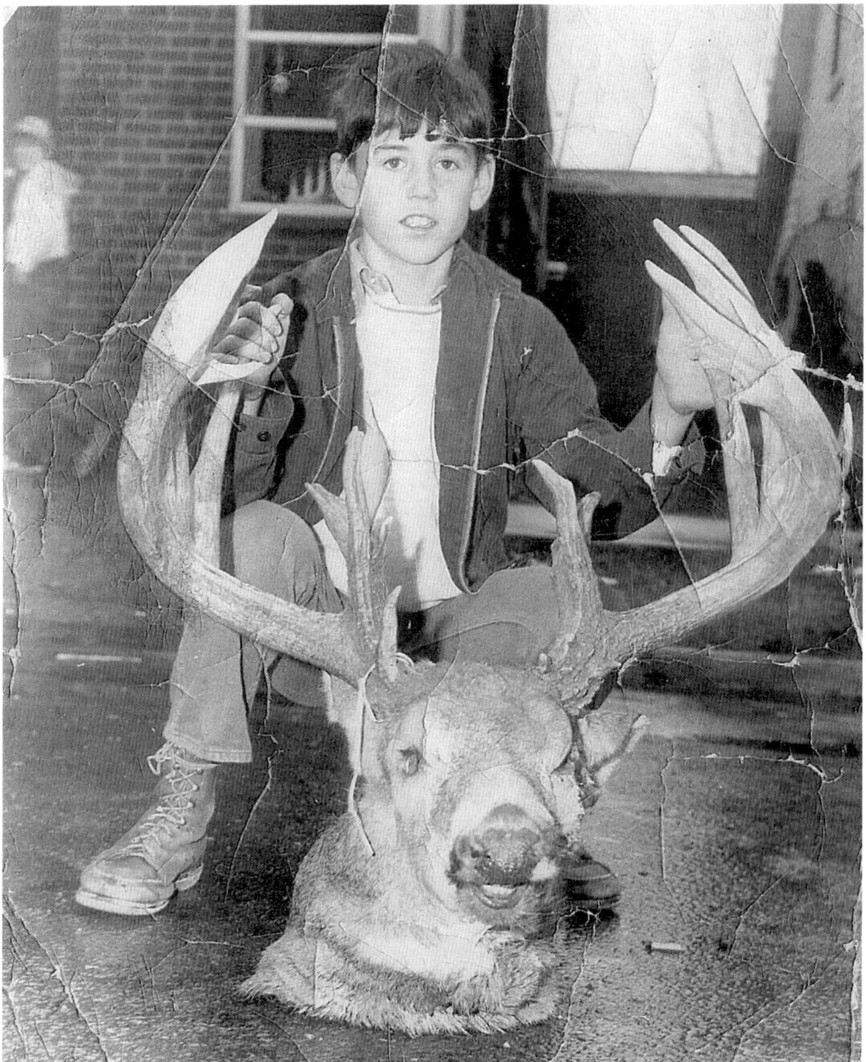

Terry Swayne and three other youngsters found this infamous buck dead in a creek. The mount now hangs in the Adams County Courthouse. *Swayne/Cross.*

hunter in southern Ohio, with the remainder of Ohio soon to follow. Tom's father hunted deer in the Roosevelt Game Preserve, now the Shawnee State Forest, with a Ted Williams Sears fiberglass longbow in the 1950s and 1960s. After scouting deer for years, it became apparent that hunters would have an advantage (as ancient hunters did) by hunting from a tree. Rope slings were devised to support the hunter entirely or serve as a back rest for lengthy hunts that commonly began hours before daylight and lasted until well after darkness had fallen. Old oak planks can still be found today, wedged between two high tree branches that once was a favored deer hunting stand.

Hunting deer over watering holes proved a successful technique. From their tree perch, Tom's father and his hunting companions would send cedar arrows tipped with three-bladed metal broadheads toward the whitetails drinking below. Another technique widely used through the early years (and to an extent today) was putting out piles of apples to create a feeding station. Baiting deer was deemed successful but took extra effort, which some didn't see as necessary as deer were being sighted often and in many numbers. What Ohio hunters realized was the whitetail's sense of smell was powerful and ended many hunts way too soon. In an attempt to hamper this advantage the deer had over the stalking or standing hunter; natural items were being experimented with. Tom's father and brothers began using apple cider and found that it worked fairly well. They poured cider over their shoes and sprinkled it around the base of the trees that held their makeshift stands overhead.

Although Tom didn't take his first deer until 1972, he was allowed to tag along on several deer hunts with his father and uncles at a young age, not carrying a gun or bow but instead a spear that young Tom had cut and sharpened himself. Tom laughed when he shared that fact with me during our interview, but the message was sincere. It was important to Tom's father that Tom would be prepared for hunting deer well before he was licensed to do so. Learning how the animal lived and reacted to various situations was vital for a boy to become a hunter. Following the elder hunting clan instilled an appreciation for not only deer hunting skills but also for the animal itself. Safe shooting with either gun or bow was as important as was placing a quick killing shot. The deer was treasured by the southwest hunters, and as the deer population grew and spread throughout the region, more people began to hunt them.

Even in the early 1960s, deer were seen often along the Ohio River counties of the southwest. Hunting was nothing new for those in the southwest, as small game hunting was commonplace. While hunting squirrels and grouse, hunters discovered deer tracks at creek crossings and along farm fields. These findings created additional excitement among small game hunters to include Ohio's big game animal to their lists of

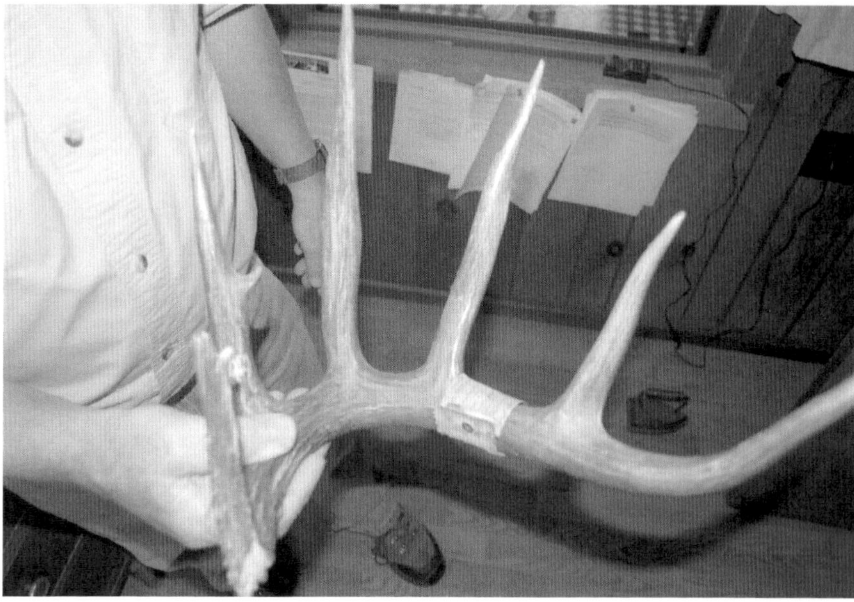

The uncle of outdoor writer Tom Cross shot this antler off a twelve-point buck during Ohio's reopening of deer seasons in 1962 in Adams County. *Robert Loewendick.*

quarry. As the 1970s arrived, the deer population in the hill country of the southwest was becoming more targeted by the growing number of hunters pursuing them. The most frequently performed hunting technique during that decade and in the next were organized deer drives. It was common for clans and groups of friends to have permission to hunt from farm to farm, forest to forest, river bottom to river bottom, in one sweep. Other than the occasional landowner declining permission, deer hunting was widely accepted and permitted by most.

The steep hills and deep ravines were best hunted by a lone hunter by still hunting. One or two steps and then wait, look and listen—this put many southwest deer hunters on course to intersect a roaming whitetail. Staking out draws was also a preferred technique that proved successful. Creek bottoms were often utilized by two deer hunters or a small group of hunters doing a well-planned deer drive. The creek bottoms served as funnel areas that deer slipped into while eluding the pushing hunter. Hunting the extremely diverse geography provided options for deer hunters through different times of the season. Bean field edges pulled deer from their wooded haunts where

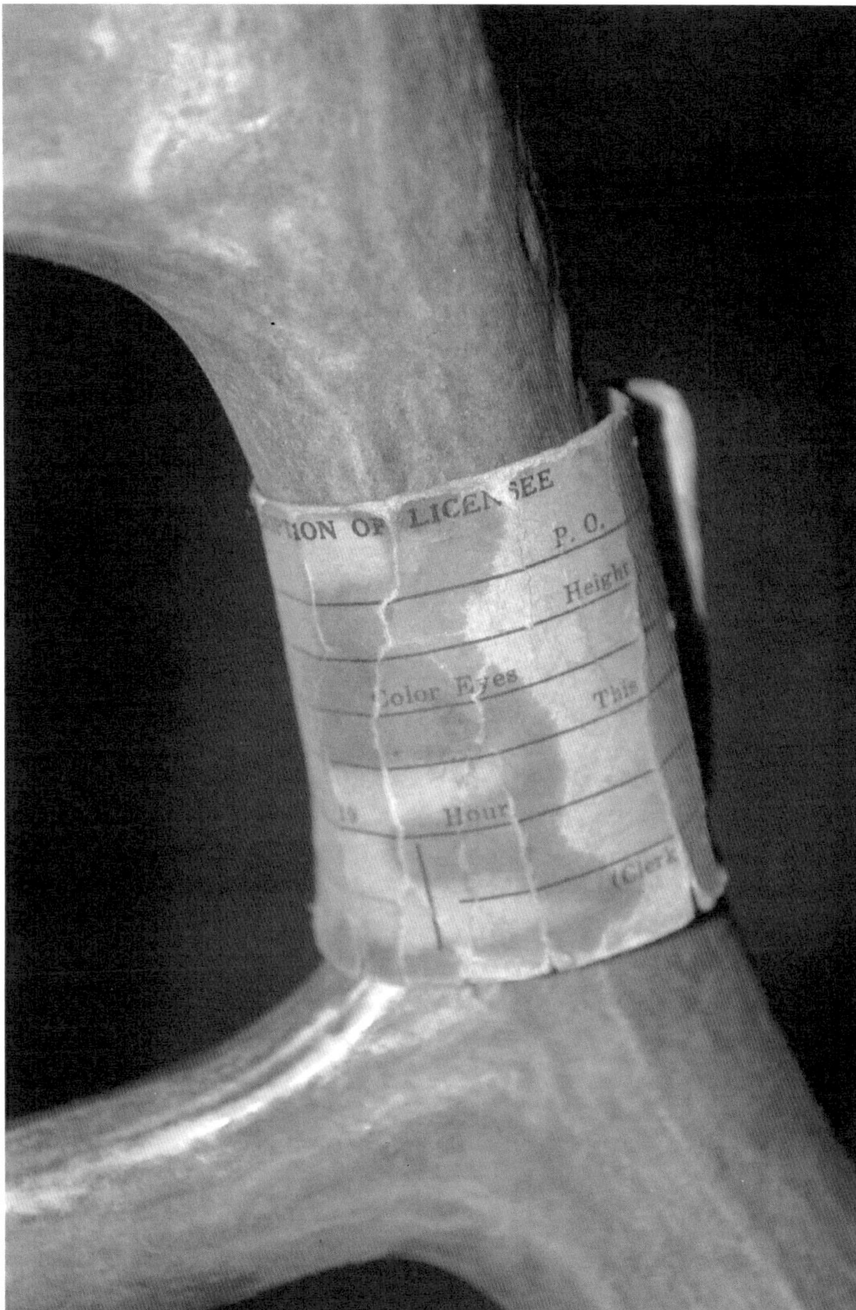

A close-up of a 1962 deer tag attached to an antler taken by Tom Cross's uncle in Adams County. *Robert Loewendick.*

hunters could take a clear shot. If the year's acorn crop was a plentiful one, then deep woods hunting was the way to go. Hunting the high ridges not found in many other regions of the state put deer hunters in position to take advantage of distant and downhill observation.

Deer hunting traditions for Tom Cross included Thanksgiving Day deer hunts with many family members. According to Tom, those hunts were more like a family reunion that involved deer hunting, telling stories about deer hunting and making plans for future deer hunts. Additional families across southwest Ohio were also involved in get-togethers focused around deer hunting. Sitting around the kitchen table, eating a hefty breakfast prepared by grandmas and daughters, was an annual treat looked forward to by many. As the family members grew older and some passed away, the group numbers began to shrink. The few who remain still try their best to continue the traditions started decades ago. While the elder and middle-aged hunters told deer hunting tales of past hunts, young prospective or active hunters absorbed the information shared. Those young hunters who are now nearing the middle-aged level themselves put forth the effort to keep a portion of the deer hunting heritage alive, but it's becoming tougher to do so as the today's youth have many recreational offerings before them.

The excitement for deer hunting is a year-round feeling among southwestern Ohio hunters. Likely, days spent afield scouting for deer outnumber the days hunting deer. Driving back roads with hopes of spotting the next whitetail legend of the southwestern Ohio River counties would quench the deer hunter's thirst for deer fun. Sitting along field edges, waiting for a whopper of a buck to reveal himself, was also often done in the summer months. Stories of big bucks and big herds traveled the counties well before deer season opened. When season was in, deer hunters often gathered at lunchtime and after dark at local establishments to share stories—both truthful and a bit spiced up. In West Union (Adams County), the 125 Grill was such a deer hunter hangout in the 1970s. If a deer story was floating around the southern counties, it would surely make a stop at the 125 Grill and similar businesses. Deer hunters from all walks of life shared time at these places, which were just another element of the camaraderie that creates a common bond among deer hunters. Deer hunters of the southern portion of the southwest displayed this as much as anywhere in the state.

Deer hunting lore varies in subject in southwest Ohio, and in talking with most deer hunters, the subject soon comes up about the trophy bucks that have come from the Ohio's southwest quarter. Trophy-sized bucks have been living and dying in the region for many decades—it's just that not all of them have been in the media's spotlight as recent trophies have. One such trophy from the past is the Old Courthouse Buck, which was found by four young boys while exploring the woods in December 1975. The twenty-seven-point buck mount was hung in the Adams County Courthouse soon after. After being refurbished and scored, the buck was returned to its position above a courthouse staircase for all to view. A more recent trophy has stepped into the limelight during the last decade—the Lucky Amish Buck. Read more about these trophies in the "Trophies" chapter.

The Flatlanders

The till plains of the southwest didn't see deer arrive regularly until the late 1970s and into the 1980s. Although the southern counties of the southwest quarter were the benefactors of the reintroduction of deer to Ohio, the northern section of the region was slow to join the ranks as serious deer hunting territory. Two hunting buddies from Greene County, Bob Brown and Mel Yearick, both traveled to the southeastern quarter of Ohio to hunt deer during the 1960s. What they learned about deer and deer hunting during those years would prove beneficial when the deer herd spread into their home county. Well experienced in small game and upland bird hunting, the two hunters were no strangers to hunting the flatlands of the northern edge of southwestern Ohio. "When we started seeing deer around here, we had to hunt them differently than we did in southeastern Ohio," said Brown. "The deer seemed to be a bit more skilled at keeping concealed from humans than their relatives we hunted years prior in Vinton County," added Yearick.

Deer would be spotted in the large agricultural fields that made up a big portion of the region's landscape. Although the deer were found, hunting for them was difficult. Just like their deer hunting comrades to the south, the northern section hunters found success with a bow and arrow. Bow hunting gave deer hunters another means to study and try to figure the incoming big game animal that was adapting to the terrain quickly. Driving deer soon became a much more successful technique to locate and drop whitetails. In 1974, it began to not be such big news to see a deer track in the mud or see one or two deer feeding along a field edge. By 1978, the deer hunting was decent.

Deer hunters who owned land or had permission from specific landowners to hunt and manage a few to several acres of land for whitetails mowed pathways to help funnel deer past the hunter's stand. From the air, the region was a collage of agricultural fields framed with fence rows and decorated with patches of woods. Clusters of cedar and CRP (Conservation Reserve Program) fields, which grow native vegetation to attract and hold wildlife, were and are common deer locations. With the wide fields providing deer the opportunity to feed out of a hunter's reach, deer hunting from a blind became more probable. Blinds placed or constructed between older-growth woodlots and fields became a deadly setup for whitetails. Because deer linger in the safe zone of a wide field, black powder rifles have become popular as a tool to reach long distances to make a killing shot. Lone drives were also a preferred method to hunt the field-roving deer, which spent much of their time within eyesight of the field when not feeding. A stealthy hunter could walk softly in the field edge, and if the cover allowed visual penetration, a deer could be spotted and stalked. All of these were typical hunting techniques used by southwest Ohio deer hunters.

Because of the bountiful agriculture fields, the deer of the region had the nutrition to grow big bodies and the bucks, massive antlers. Two trophy bucks taken during the last decade, the Mike Beatty Buck and the Brad Jerman Buck, are perfect representatives of this. Read more about them in the "Trophies" chapter. Reports of deer weighing more than two hundred pounds were a common event. Road kills in the late 1970s involved trophy-sized deer, both bucks and does. The northern portion of the southwest is in the creating stage of building deer hunting traditions. A fair amount of whitetails are providing decent hunting today across the area, and local deer hunters have a legitimate shot at not only a big-bodied deer but maybe a trophy in the antler department as well.

Veteran outdoorsman Keith Linkhart, also of Greene County, has enjoyed the addition of white-tailed deer to his part of Ohio. "My father, brother and I hunted deer in Pennsylvania in the early '50s," said Linkhart. "We hunted fox and small game around home quite a lot before the deer showed up in the late '70s. After that, we had another hunting option, which was welcome." Although deer may not have been plentiful before the 1970s, this doesn't mean that they weren't there. In the early 1940s, Linkhart came

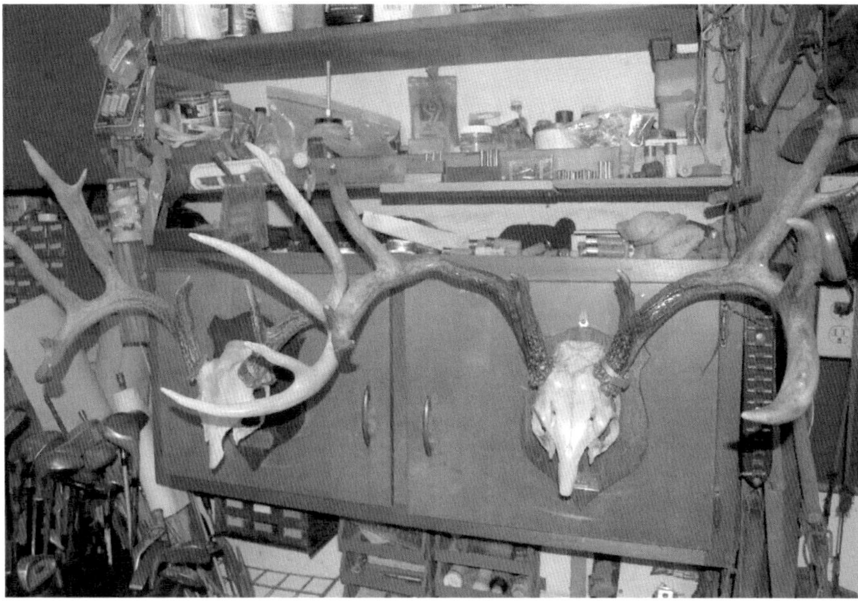

Heavy-antlered bucks are nothing new, as these pair of racks show, taken before designated food plots and antler-enhancing supplements became widely used. *Robert Loewendick.*

across a deer track in the mud while fox hunting. He followed the tracks for a short distance before losing them. Three years later, he saw a deer on his farm for the first time. Linkhart's father offered some advice for the young fox hunter who was about to begin hunting deer on their farm:

> *Hunting deer takes patience. Extreme patience. To see deer, get settled in comfortably in a location where you are confident they will visit. Sit there until you can't stand it any longer and then sit there for two more hours.*

The terrain in the northeast corner of the southwest region is similar to the portion of the quarter to the west. Whitetails have reached the carrying capacity of the available habitat according to some landowners and regional hunters. I met an interesting senior hunter while researching the region, and his name is Karl Wilburn. Karl's knowledge of deer and deer hunting in this region was impressive, to say the least. Karl saw the first deer in his region of the state in January 1955 near Cedarville, when deer in that part of Ohio was not unheard of. Later in 1960, he saw a deer scamper across the road

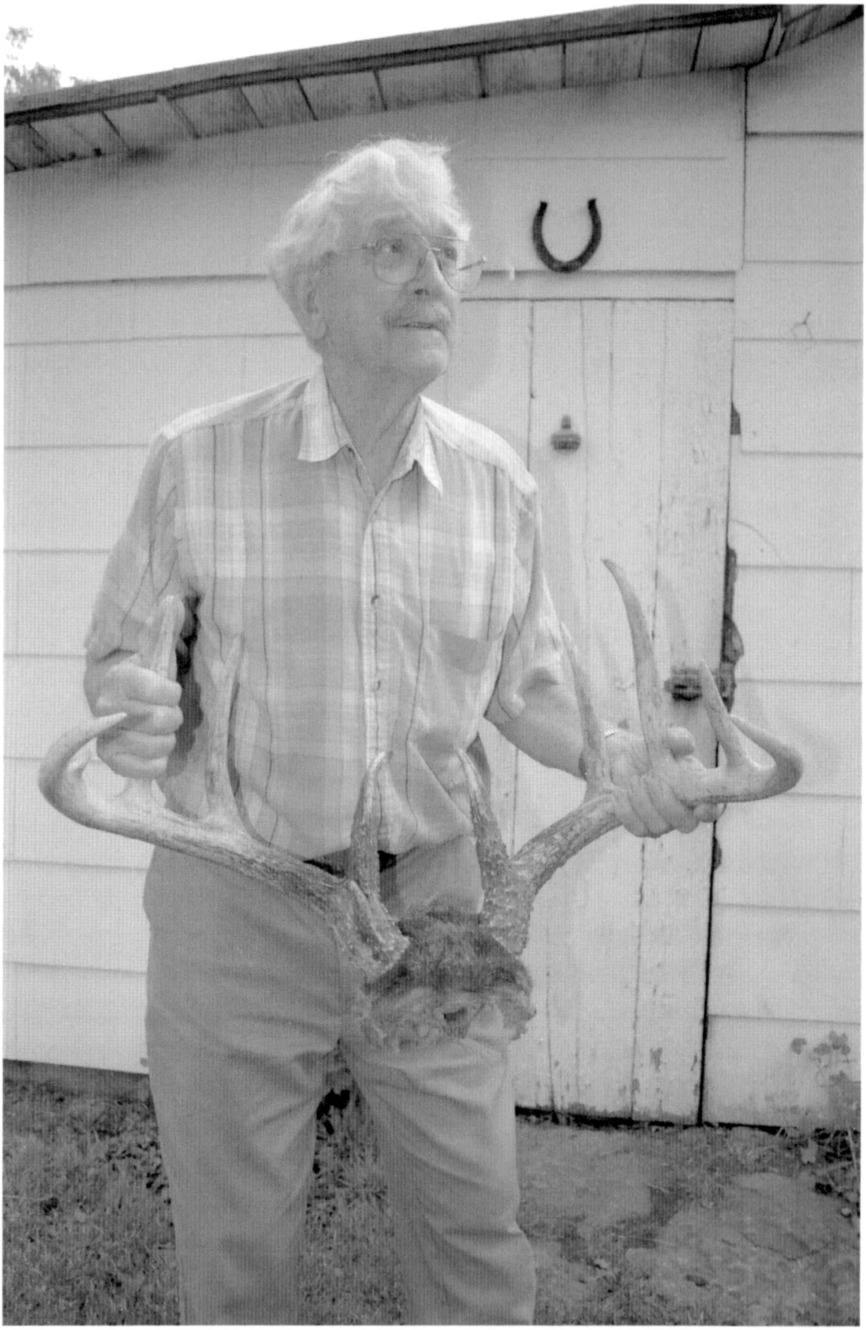

Karl Wilburn's buck proves that good hunting was had in the early 1970s as Ohio's deer populations spread to the southern and western regions of the state. *Robert Loewendick.*

in front of his vehicle. In 1978, Karl spotted the first deer on his farm. He had seen tracks in the mud earlier but thought that they had been left by an escaped hog. Since then, Karl has taken many (no exact number recorded) deer with gun and bow.

The largest antlered buck Karl has killed qualified and was entered in the Buckeye Big Buck Club. Deer of that region offered the same hunting challenges as the western portion did and does, with a hodgepodge of ag fields and woodlots tagged together with tree and fence rows. Hunting deer living among that landscape was more challenging than hunting big woods, or big woods with an adjoining field. The deer living there seemed to be a bit slyer than deer Karl had hunted in Michigan and other parts of Ohio. A specific deer that Karl hunted for five seasons represents the tenacity of the deer and deer hunting the northern edge of the southwest quarter of Ohio. Following is the story of that five-year quest for the deer with an extra white chin.

Glassing a field that attracted nice bucks in the past, Karl spotted a set of antlers sticking up a several inches more than the tallest vegetation. The buck was exceptionally handsome, Karl thought. He put the binoculars to his eyes, studied the buck's face and then lowered the binoculars to focus on the memorization. The buck had an identifying marking: an extra-long white stripe on his chin that nearly reached his bright white throat patch. Later that autumn, Karl was sitting in his tree stand along a small woodlot with a fence row leading away from it and splitting two bean fields as the white-chinned buck approached. Karl was excited to see the beautiful buck again. Karl was so fixed on observing the buck that he nearly drew the arrow too late. He did draw the arrow but it missed its mark. Later, during the same archery season, Karl had a second opportunity at the buck, and the same result ensued.

The following spring while shed hunting, Karl saw two does standing in a field close by. After getting a better look at the does, it became evident that one of the does was actually the white-chinned buck with bloody pedicles, which his antlers were recently attached to. Karl and the buck stood staring at each other, sizing each other's competitor up possibly. Then the buck slipped away. The following autumn, Karl was hunting over a swamp that showed signs of multiple deer using the area. The rut was on, and Karl was sure that he would see white chin again, if the deer survived the summer and hadn't been taken by another bow hunter by now. A two-year-old buck came through the swamp chasing a fork horn from the territory. The ten-pointer returned to the location moments later and approached Karl's tree stand.

Not being the white-chinned buck Karl was looking for, he let the ten-pointer pass. The buck hung around Karl's stand, offering several shooting opportunities, which tempted Karl to take this deer. Karl held his bow as if he was preparing to shoot but never pulled an arrow. The ten-pointer lingered longer, even chewed and rubbed his eye glands on the tip of a branch that was at the base of the tree that held Karl and his stand. The buck worked his scrape for a few more moments. Karl continued to resist taking a shot. As darkness fell, Karl met his wife at the road at a predetermined location. As Karl was loading his gear into the car, he heard a shot back in the direction of his stand. The next morning, Karl found bloodstained drag marks leading from a field onto the road. He followed the blood trail to a small gut pile, likely that of a yearling, the work of poachers. Karl became concerned that the poachers might have taken the white-chinned buck also, as it had been some time since he had seen the special buck.

The third gun season since observing the white-chinned buck, Karl was once again perched in his tree stand. Soon after hearing shots on a neighboring farm, he saw a buck running along a fence row, heading toward Karl. It was the white-chinned buck. For Karl, it was like seeing an old friend after years of absence. The fence row skirted a soy bean stubble field with some tall weeds against the fence. Karl frantically searched visually left and right, not seeing the buck and wondering where he would go. Moments passed, and it was as if the buck had sunk into the ground and disappeared. No sign of the buck, so Karl left for lunch. Upon Karl's return to the tree stand after lunch, he was surprised by the white-chinned buck as it jumped up from its bed. The buck must have lain down and stayed low enough in the vegetation that Karl was not able to spot him before leaving his stand.

Karl fired a shot at the fleeing buck. The buck rolled as the bullet penetrated him. Assuming he had hit the deer's spine, Karl readied for a second shot in case it was needed. It was. The buck rolled over on his stomach and began pulling himself along with his two front feet. He soon was on all four feet and moving once again. The buck crossed several properties, and Karl followed in pursuit. Karl never caught up with the buck, and when the little blood trail tapered off, Karl had begun to wonder if the buck was going to survive. This event occurred on the last day of season. Late the next spring, Karl observed two bucks together in a bean field. One prolonged stare revealed to Karl that one of the bucks was the white-chinned acquaintance. He had survived.

The next deer season, Karl was positioned not far from a power line tower that was in the middle of a field. Karl observed a few does and their fawns feeding about. Something near the base of the tower caught Karl's attention. It was the white-chinned buck, and he was watching the does. Karl watched the actions taking place, hoping to get another chance at the mature deer. He was watching the does when they spooked and trotted off. Karl turned to look to see the buck's reaction to the does, and he was gone. Karl heard the buck grunt while exerting effort to jump a fence, the similar sound an overweight person would make trying to jump rope. Karl was sure that the buck weighed near three hundred pounds.

As before, the buck was headed toward Karl's stand and sneaking along the fence line doing so. Within shooting range, the buck stopped with brush between him and the hunter who had hunted him for the last five deer seasons. Karl could see him standing there, nose in the air, picking up Karl's scent for sure. The white-chinned buck turned and walked away the same way it came in. Karl never saw the buck again and never heard of anyone tagging him in at a checking station.

Chapter 6

THE SOUTHEAST

Ohio's southeastern quarter has been considered the white-tailed deer hunting capital of the state for decades. With the reintroduction of deer to Ohio occurring at the southwestern edge of this quarter, it wasn't long before deer were creeping into the southeast's hill country. From the northern edge of the southeast quarter, the deer that had moved in from Pennsylvania were now turning south and joining the growing herd there. The terrain that welcomed the migrating deer herds was prime for growing and sustaining a healthy and numerous deer population.

The southeast region of Ohio is a deer hunter's paradise that is similar to most of Ohio in the diversity category. From the gorges of the Hocking Hills region to the hills that skirt the Ohio River, and from the flatlands of the central Ohio portion to the rises and valleys decorated with lakes and mature forests, it comes together to create a scenic region in which to pursue the whitetail. The Wayne National Forest boundaries encompass more than 833,990 acres, most of which are privately owned. But the public acres that do exist are composed of wild lands and waters that possibly hold the best deer hunting opportunities in the state.

One interstate highway runs north and south through the eastern portion of the southeast, but access to Ohio's popular deer lands was easily accomplished by the well-maintained state and county roads. Most of the two-lane roads are somewhat winding and lead campers up and down as they travel this hilly section. For deer hunters wanting to "get away from it all," the southeast quarter provides a touch of the wilderness feel. With hills and hollows come waterfalls, caves and rivers, which add to the adventurous theme that some deer hunters prefer. The flora of southeastern Ohio is diverse, with species growing there that are normally found in Canada, brought about by the presence of glaciers thousands of years ago. Hemlocks and rhododendrons are commonly found anchored in the deep, cool gorges and along hills and sharp ridge tops. This region may be the most scenic in Ohio for the deer hunter to enjoy his time in the natural world.

Throughout the 1970s and 1980s, southeast Ohio was in the national spotlight regarding modern-day deer hunting. My home county, Muskingum, benefited immensely from the economic boost that deer hunters provided while staying for the weeklong deer season. Surrounding counties also reaped financial benefits from the visiting deer hunters, many of whom were nonresidents. During recent seasons, it was noted to me by a wildlife biologist that Ohio has regularly sold nonresident hunting and deer tags to citizens from every state but Hawaii. During those booming years, it was the mix of the abundant deer population, big-antlered bucks and the thousands of public hunting acres. The entire southeastern quarter experienced the influx of deer hunters to some extent throughout the period. Today, as most private lands were accessible for hunting if the landowner was asked, they have either been sold to housing developers or leased by financially secure individuals or groups. However, most of the thousands of public hunting acres that were available beginning in the 1930s are still open to the public today. The ODNR's Division of Wildlife is steadily applying the efforts to obtain and manage new land by either donation or use of funds donated by individuals. These efforts should secure first-class deer hunting opportunities well into the future.

I Saw a Deer Track!

A decade after the first deer hunt occurred in Ohio during the twentieth century, which included only three counties, southeastern Ohio was gearing up to become Ohio's deer and deer hunter magnet. My grandfather and two uncles, avid outdoorsmen involved in any type of hunting that was available, would make the annual trip to Pennsylvania to hunt the famous deer herds of the 1940s. Even into the early 1950s, their deer hunting efforts were focused

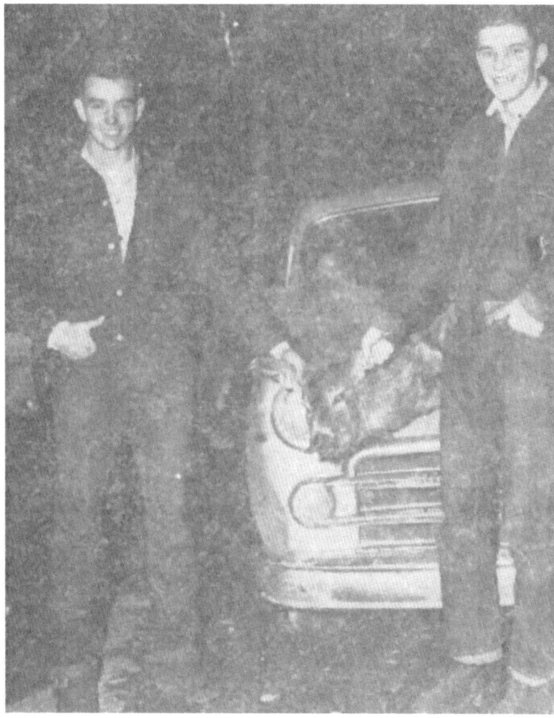

The author's uncle and uncle's friend pose with one of the first deer taken in Muskingum County in 1956. Only 3,911 were taken in Ohio that year. *Robert Loewendick.*

across the state line. The younger of the two uncles, Jim Berry, was just entering his teen years as the mid-century mark appeared on the calendar. In 1956, Uncle Jim became involved in Ohio's developing deer hunting heritage at the age of seventeen. Like a few southeastern Ohio outdoorsmen of the 1950s, Jim had discovered a set of deer tracks. Deer tracks began showing up occasionally throughout the forests and fields of the southeast that had supported small game hunting for decades. The tracks were seen, but hardly ever was the deer that left its mark in the mud.

On a 1956 December trapping line inspection, Jim steered his small boat powered by a two-horsepower engine upstream on the Licking River in western Muskingum County. The Licking River was flanked by woodlands and some open but weedy fields. Surveying his surroundings as he went, watching for furbearer sign and other game, Jim saw a deer track among other wildlife tracks on the riverbank. He pulled the boat to shore and tied off to an exposed root. The surprise of finding a deer track was exciting enough, but what if he could find the deer that made it? That would be a story to tell for weeks. Jim crawled out of the boat to have a better look.

A moment later, he heard movement in the brush farther up the brush-covered hillside. He froze. He strained to see what made the sound and where it was exactly. He saw nothing. He shrugged off the incident and reentered his boat.

He shoved off and started the small engine. He throttled up to regain the upstream course when movement on the hillside caught his attention. Three deer stood near one another, watching Jim going up the river. Seeing the deer was nearly more excitement than the seventeen-year-old could stand. He couldn't wait to get home to tell his buddies at school. The following day, Jim purchased a deer license and planned to add his Mossberg bolt-action shotgun to his trapping gear in the boat. "How cool would that be if I could take one of those deer?" Jim asked himself over and over.

As Jim approached the spot along the riverbank where he had seen the deer and the deer tracks, his eyes scanned the hillside searching for the slightest movement. From hunting deer in Pennsylvania with his brother and father, he had learned just how skittish a white-tailed deer was. Jim nosed his boat onshore once again. He loaded the shotgun with three shells and began to walk up the river as quietly as he could. Each step sounded to him like a drum being hit. Each flutter of a shed leaf rustling against another or being run over by a chipmunk increased the excitement being restrained by the teenager. His hearing was on high alert, and every sound he heard was surely one of the deer moving about—or so he thought.

Patience was one attribute Jim learned by spending hundreds of hours in the woods hunting small game. As hunting wild animals does regularly, lessons are taught nearly every time a hunter enters a field or woods. His patience would be tested this day if he was looking for a deer. There had been fewer than one hundred deer killed in the entire county that year. Jim had heard older guys talking about seeing a deer, and if he could bring one home, it would surely be an accomplishment by a young hunter. But first he must locate one of those deer he saw a couple of days prior.

The cool December air was seasonably pleasant. A nice day for a hunt, Jim thought. Other thoughts were running around in his head when his next footstep spooked the bedded deer into standing up. The doe hesitated for only a couple seconds before fleeing up and across the hillside. Jim pulled his shotgun up and pulled the trigger while leading the doe with the gun barrel. The gun did not fire. He tugged at the trigger a second time and a third. No fire. He switched his focus from the running deer to the nonfiring shotgun.

He soon realized that the safety was still on. In his haste to get a shot off at this rarely seen big game animal, he forgot to slip the safety off. He quickly tried to center the sight on the deer again, but as he found the deer in his line of sight, it disappeared over a newly constructed railroad track bed.

Jim ran, with the safety back on, up to the last place he saw the doe. She left tracks on the new railroad bed but no sign further than that. Jim sat and waited for the deer to reappear and hoped that he would have the great deer hunting story he dreamed of come true, instead of a tale about the one that got away. He hunted for the doe for several minutes more, but he saw nothing. Where was she now? Could she be circling back around? Or is she high-tailing it to the next valley? All Jim could think about was the missed opportunity, so he headed back to the boat without his deer.

Jim sat in the boat for a while and sulked. He couldn't believe what had happened. After some further thought, he decided to go back up the hill and have one more look. He understood the uniqueness of the opportunity and wanted to have another crack at it. Up and over the railroad bed and down the other side he went. He crossed a small creek, and before reaching the other side, the doe jumped up from her new hiding spot. This time the safety on the gun was not forgotten. He quickly shouldered the shotgun and fired. The doe dropped. Jim approached slowly, all the while hoping that she wouldn't stand and escape a second time. She didn't.

Jim dragged the field-dressed doe to the point where he had to get her over a fence. The doe proved to be too much of a challenge for the scrawny kid to clear the obstacle between him and the boat that would deliver the news and proof of his finding deer tracks along the Licking River. After deciding on a new course, he dragged the doe through the small creek that led to the river. He pulled the deer into the boat with a heave and ho, and downriver he went as fast as the two-horsepower engine could push water. After arriving at his car, he loaded the deer and headed to town. In Zanesville, he stopped at the local newspaper office, where he was photographed by a staff photographer. The photo of Uncle Jim and a friend, and the doe from the Licking River bottomlands, was displayed in the newspaper the next day.

Jim told and retold his first Ohio deer hunting story for weeks after the picture appeared. One person who was not impressed with the newspaper photo was Jim's high school principal. It seems that Jim had skipped school that day to pursue the white-tailed deer he had seen while running his trapline. Because of that, a few afternoons were spent in detention at

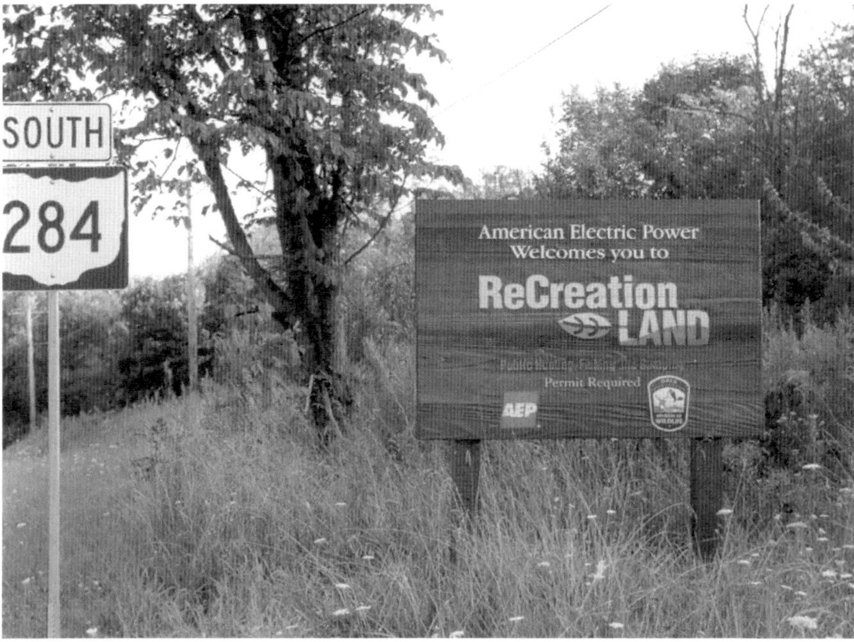

Ohio's public hunting lands, such as the AEP Recreational Lands in southeast Ohio, have provided quality deer hunting for half a century. *Robert Loewendick.*

school, but according to Jim, it was all worth it. The only concern Jim had about spending time after school during hunting and trapping season was that the time wasted inside cost him valuable time in the woods and on the river in pursuit of his next adventure. And with more deer starting to call southeastern Ohio home, deer hunting adventures would continue to grow as well.

The northern central portion of the southeast quarter was the focus of multiple outdoor media outlets covering Ohio's expanding deer herd. During the 1960s, the deer herd was steadily growing in numbers—not exploding but slowly getting setting a solid foothold in the region. When the 1970s arrived, things were getting busier in the deer hunting world throughout the southeast. Different from the 1960s, when deer hunting was more of quiet sport entering the culture, the 1970s was beginning to see Ohio deer hunting's business side. As more impressive deer hunting stories were published, the more deer hunters would journey to the area.

On the southern stretch of the southeastern Ohio quarter, in Washington County, veteran whitetail hunter Percy Hill has been participating in Ohio's deer season regularly since 1943. Missing only two deer seasons (because of his commitment to his country by serving in the military), Hill has seen Ohio's deer hunting come full circle. The rugged hills that lie just northeast of Marietta are included in a section of the Wayne National Forest. The Ohio River town of New Matamoras was an area that held a few deer worthy of hunting in the 1940s and 1950s. Hill and his father hunted that area, which was traversed by the Little Muskingum River. The landscape was primarily wooded, with pasture lands intermixed. Hill's father killed a buck sporting antlers that qualified for entry into the Buckeye Big Buck Club in 1952. The senior Hill's buck was one of the charter entries of the club.

With so much deer habitat in place throughout the southern lands, deer hunters didn't have to travel north and west to hunt deer, as they had a realistic, huntable herd close to home. However, when a deer was discovered on a property and the story spread of its existence there, numerous hunters would show up to pursue the animal. Early on, it was best if a deer hunter kept a deer sighting to himself to avoid drawing competition. In 1957, the Hills, father and son, took one deer each and with only an hour between kills. This was an amazing accomplishment at the time, since deer were still establishing their presence. The following season, which was only two days long, the Hills only saw six deer. As the 1970 seasons opened, deer were seen more regularly. Although more deer were there for the taking, hunting them was still labor intensive. According to Hill, sitting in stands waiting for a deer to lumber past was hardly heard of in the southeast. The deer of the southeast didn't have the need to travel longer distances to find food sources and watering sites. Therefore, organized deer drives were what it took to get deer stirring around to improve the hunter's chances of taking a deer. Through the last three decades, the landscape changed, which increased deer habitat, and the deer responded well.

Farther to the west, around Jackson and Athens, deer hunting had been the focus of numerous hunters beginning in the late 1940s. Deer hunters from around the state considered this portion of the southeast region as the only place in the state worth visiting to hunt deer. A senior hunter told me how he chose Vinton County as an area to explore for deer hunting possibilities in the late 1940s and early 1950s. He spread out an Ohio road map on his table and searched for an area that had the fewest roads. His fingertip pegged a spot on the map in the Wayne National Forest. Many older deer hunters across the state revealed to me during interviews for this book that Vinton

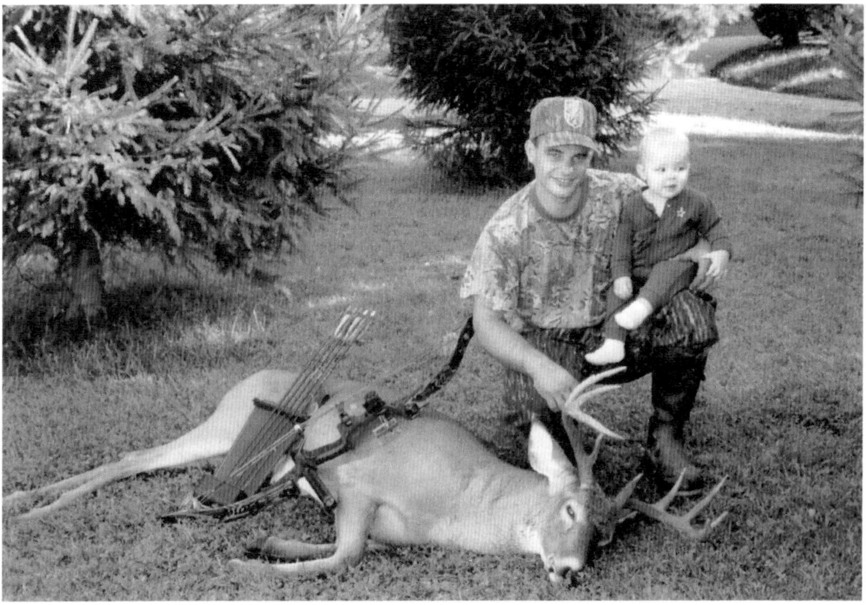

Deer hunting the hills of southeastern Ohio has been passed on from generation to generation. The author's nephew, Joe Dutro, and Joe's daughter, Abbey, are here with a trophy. *Robert Loewendick.*

County and surrounding counties were the places to find deer during those early seasons. Not only were quality deer there and somewhat numerous, the residents of the area were also receptive to incoming hunters. The hospitality offered by many of the Vinton County folks was appreciated by most visiting hunters. It was not uncommon for landowners to agree to allowing deer hunters to set up camp at the rear of their properties. Gracious landowners were also great sources for locating deer.

THE PRESSURE IS ON

Swinging back toward the center of the southeast quarter, two specific areas are found that also have been popular targets for deer hunters: the Blue Rock State Forest and the American Electric Power (AEP) Recreational Lands (formally known as the Ohio Power Lands). The Blue Rock State Forest was the site of early deer research programs. The reforestation projects performed throughout the 1940s to increase forestland in Ohio also turned out to be an effort appreciated by the white-tailed deer and deer hunters. A few miles to the southeast of Blue Rock lies the AEP Recreational Lands, which cover thirty thousand mildly rugged acres that were surfaced mined for coal. Nearly 380 campsites organized in several campgrounds accommodate deer hunters taking advantage of the wildness style of deer hunting today. The reclaimed mine lands began attracting deer soon after the process of returning the land to a naturally productive state had begun.

During the 1970s, deer hunting throughout this region was becoming a subject that would soon be a force to be reckoned with. According to Jerry Wade of Nashport, a retired wildlife enforcement supervisor for the Ohio Division of Wildlife, the quality deer herd established in the region had created the need for increased wildlife law enforcement. During the deer gun seasons of the 1970s and 1980s, wildlife officers from Ohio counties that had very few deer would be transferred to the region for the busy gun week to assist local officers. The most common problem on the law enforcement side was hunters hunting on private lands without permission. Calls to officers regarding spotlighting deer at night were also on the rise. Wade said that the deer hunters moving to southeast Ohio were not looking

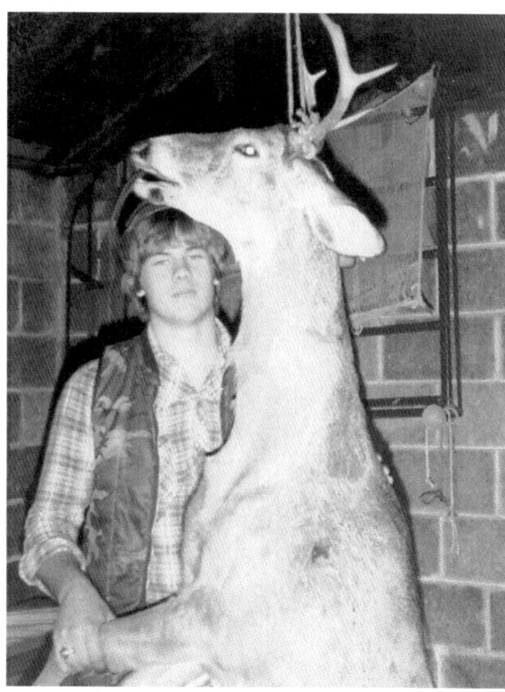

The author's cousin, Joe Walpole, stands proudly with his first buck. This deer was taken in Muskingum County in 1977. *Joe Walpole.*

for trouble; they simply wanted to have a shot at a trophy buck. Most wildlife law enforcement confrontations were handled without any dilemma. Deer hunting was taking on a new appearance in Ohio, and the southeastern quarter was seeing it firsthand.

The southeast was the home of a large number of public hunting acres in nearly every county of the region. Access was not a problem, and there was plenty of room to roam—for both the deer and the deer hunter. Following the busy and numerous mining operations, the second-growth forests and brushy habitats created during reclamation offered prime deer hunting. During the gun seasons, it was common to see out-of-state license plates on vehicles frequenting the small towns of the region. The southeastern counties that were in the media spotlight continued to see lots of deer hunting pressure. Wade believes that the reason so many deer were taken from the region was not only because of the available deer herd but also simply because

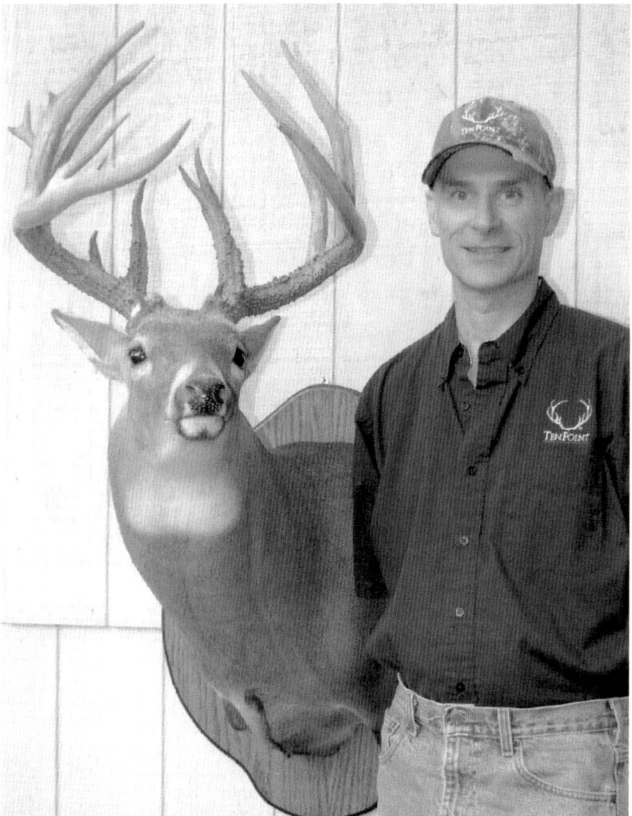

Bucks sporting antlers like this Muskingum County trophy set, taken by Gil Gard of Hopewell, attracted hunters from near and far during the 1980s and 1990s. *Robert Loewendick.*

more hunters were hunting there compared to other regions of the state. As the hunting pressure began to spread across the state, Wade's belief was supported by those other counties earning higher harvest numbers. Wade added that once a few trophy bucks are taken from a particular area, the pressure will surely arrive. Today, this is the case in southwest Ohio after several record-breaking bucks have been publicized heavily.

The 1990s welcomed even more deer hunters to the southeast quarter as the deer population was reaching its highest total of the century. Deer hunters who hunted the region through the earlier decades often returned for reasons of traditions or because they had lost access to hunting grounds close to their homes. Deer management practices were being tested during this decade, and more liberal seasons worked to reduce the blossoming deer herd. The hunters were still coming, but soon they would begin to look at other regions of Ohio to hunt as big buck stories came forth. Currently, deer management plans are focused on maintaining a quality herd and working at reducing the deer numbers in urban areas, where they have become a common sight and a nuisance. Trophy bucks are still regularly harvested here and are exposed on the pages of hunting magazines—which, as before, attracts some hunters, but not as many as the two previous decades had. The southeastern quarter will continue to be a popular location for deer hunters as the abundance of public hunting lands and the wildness flavor of the region remains intact.

Chapter 7

TROPHIES

Ohio's white-tailed deer hunting legacy is decorated with loads of trophy-sized bucks. The definition of a trophy regarding deer depends on the individual hunter. An old, wise doe that eluded hunters for multiple years should be considered a trophy. A hunter's first deer is considered a trophy. But the trophies discussed in this chapter are defined as such because of the large size of their antlers. For many deer hunters, a trophy antlered buck is why they spend the time and money to hunt them. Much more so now than fifty years ago, the amount of money spent on researching and scouting, gaining access to lands, travel expenses and missed wages is unbelievable. The price to pursue a trophy buck can get expensive, but for dedicated trophy hunters it's all worth the effort.

The lands that supported the reintroduced deer herd to Ohio in the 1940s were not managed specifically for growing huge racks of antlers on bucks. It was as it was. As the attraction to big bucks grew across Ohio, so did the desires of trophy hunters to create landscapes to lure and hold big deer for hunting. From simply mowing a few paths around heavy cover to planting specific vegetation to provide deer, producing trophy bucks was beginning to be big business in the 1990s and is even bigger today.

Serious trophy buck hunters learned early on that simply showing up on opening day of whatever season they participated in and plopping down in the woods or field was not going to work. Oh sure, there have been hundreds of big bucks taken across Ohio by first-time hunters or fair-weather hunters.

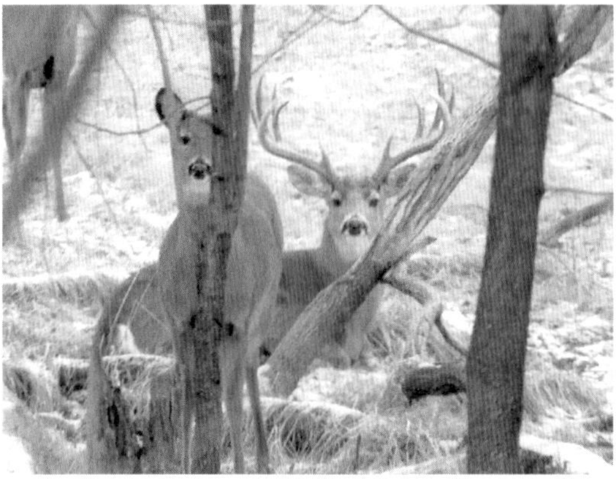

Huge antlered, mature bucks are what many deer hunters' dreams are made of. *Robert Loewendick.*

But to consistently have a chance to see an old wily buck or even have a shot at him was a four-season event. Scouting during the spring, summer and early fall would increase the odds of the committed trophy hunter when hunting season opened. During the early decades of Ohio's deer seasons, nowhere near the effort to take a trophy buck was made. For the most part, when a big antlered buck was killed during the earlier seasons, it was a pleasant surprise for not only the hunter but also for those hearing the story or seeing the deer.

A modern representation as to the astounding value of what a trophy buck is today is revealed by the ODNR's Division of Wildlife's revised restitution law for illegal taking of white-tailed deer. For example, a recent deer poacher was sentenced for his crime. Here are a few highlights from a DOW press release regarding the case:

> *A Scioto County man pled guilty to four wildlife violations in Adams County Court on Friday, April 30, 2010 and was ordered to pay $23,572.05 in restitution, according to the Ohio Department of Natural Resources (ODNR), Division of Wildlife. The man pled guilty to four charges including taking a deer in a closed season, hunting without permission, no hunting license and no deer permit. The judge presiding over the case ordered the man to pay $1,500 in fines, an additional $134 court costs, and to forfeit the deer as well as the bow he used to kill it. In addition, he will lose his hunting privileges for life. He also had ten prior wildlife convictions for deer violations and has spent time in jail for several of those offenses. He will be entered into the Wildlife Violator's Compact and most likely will lose hunting rights in 33 other states.*

> *...The Division of Wildlife is also imposing restitution for the deer in the amount of $23,572.05. This is in accordance with Ohio's revised restitution law for illegal taking of white-tailed deer. The law went into effect March 2008 and allows the Division of Wildlife to seek an increased recovery value on all illegally harvested wildlife. The typical trophy deer, scored according to Boone & Crockett (B&C) guidelines, netted an impressive 197 2/8. This deer was the largest typical white-tailed deer harvested in North America during 2009. In Ohio, this deer would rank fourth all time in the Buckeye Big Buck Club records.*
>
> *...The recovery value for individual white-tailed deer is derived from the formula listed in 1531.201 of the Ohio Revised Code. The value is determined by measuring the antlers and using the following formula plus the value derived for wildlife. The formula for white-tailed deer will be applied to all individuals whose gross score exceeds 125 Boone and Crockett (B&C) inches. The formula is: Recovery Value = [(gross score—100)2 x $1.65] + the value derived in the Wildlife Value Formula ($500 as of 3/08).*

It's clear by these efforts by the DOW to reclaim a trophy buck's value that a trophy buck today is much more than a wall decoration. Multiple businesses have been created because of the appeal that trophy deer hunting has gained. The deer hunting gear manufacturing industry has become a booming trade. Hunting tools by the hundreds have arrived on the market to assist would-be and serious trophy hunters alike in harvesting one of Ohio's extremely valuable large-antlered bucks. Ohio's trophies compete well in the scoring game with any state or providence in North America. Add to that fact the reality of a substantial deer herd supporting up to six deer harvests per hunter per season in the largest regulated deer zone, and it becomes evident as to why Ohio is a leading trophy deer state.

Numerous trophy bucks have qualified for various record books and have had their stories well published and mounts on display for thousands to see. But what about the hundreds of trophy bucks that never had their antlers measured and scored to confirm their record book validity? Although antler scoring has been around since the 1940s, the enthusiasm to have a deer scored was not as widespread as it seems today. And it's safe to say that there were trophy-sized bucks roaming Ohio back then that easily would have

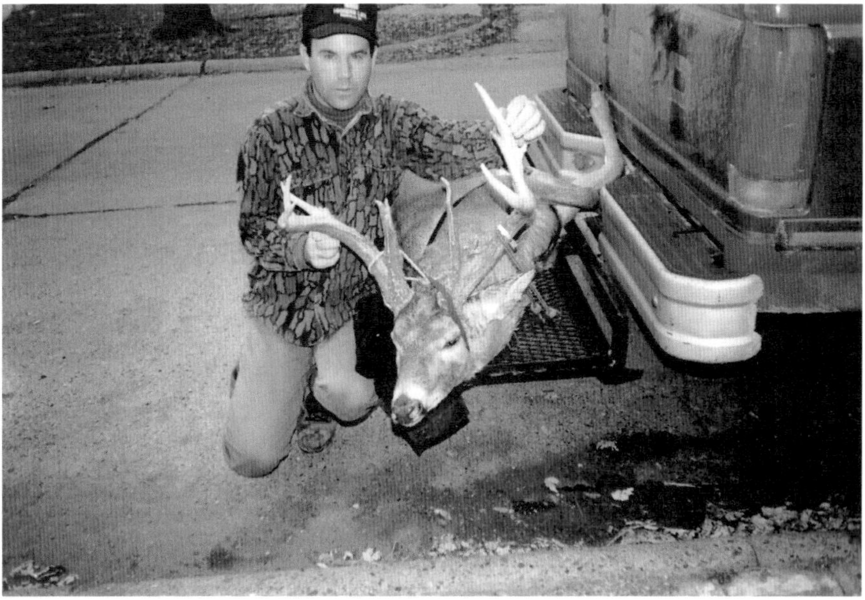

Many trophy-sized bucks like Russ Faulhaber's southeastern Ohio buck were not photographed, which led to many worthy trophies not getting recognized. *Russ Faulhaber.*

made today's requirements for record book entry—not as many as today, with the much higher deer populations and abundance of nutrition gained from agriculture, but trophy bucks just the same. I've heard many trophy buck stories from around the state, and when asked if the buck was ever scored and entered into the Buckeye Big Buck Club (BBBC), the reply was often, "Nope. Just hung the antlers in the garage or barn as a reminder of the big guy and exciting moment when I took him." One interview turned up a story of a man who shot a trophy deer in the late 1990s. The hunter was questioned by many if he had poached the big buck or if he had actually hit it with his vehicle and simply wanted the fame of being a trophy hunter. The hunter repeatedly assured the doubters that he shot it, as he claimed the day he did it. The hunter was a reputable man and well liked in the community. After a couple months of the harassment, the hunter told several acquaintances that he was sorry that he ever shot the big deer. It wasn't worth the hassle.

A Sampling of Ohio's Trophy Bucks

According to Mike Rex—past president of the BBBC and the hunter who arrowed a non-typical trophy buck in 2005 that wore seventeen points with fifteen-inch brow tines and scored 218 6/8—the past twenty years have been Ohio's trophy buck primetime. Rex believes that with Ohio being such a bargain for nonresident hunters to have a legitimate shot at a world-class buck, and due to an increase of both resident and nonresidents participating in the lengthy archery season, entries into the BBBC will not slow anytime soon. Rex applauds Ohio's deer managers for encouraging deer hunters to harvest does and not allowing gun hunting during the rut. Because of these two facts, Ohio's bucks are able to mature and grow trophy-caliber antlers.

Thousands of Ohio's big-antlered bucks have been entered into record books of the BBBC and other bookkeeping organizations. Each county (some much more than others) of the state has given up a trophy-sized buck at one time or another by this point. As stated before, some hunters consider an antler's score something to behold, and some appreciate impressive antler sets without needing to know what the total inches are. Either way, a trophy buck is something to admire, and through the remainder of this chapter, a selection of a few notables are highlighted. The following trophies are just an example of the type of deer bringing notoriety to Ohio as a trophy deer state. The first two trophies to follow are Ohio's best hunter-taken bucks in two categories on record to date.

The Beatty Buck

Mike Beatty of Xenia arrowed a thirty-nine-point non-typical buck on November 8, 2000, in Greene County. The massive antlered buck would eventually be scored at 304 6/8—the largest deer taken by a hunter in the world. Beatty believed that he saw the buck three weeks prior to the day he killed the world record, but he wasn't sure. Prior to this buck, Beatty considered himself a meat hunter first and foremost and a buck hunter second. Beatty said that he was fortunate and blessed to be sitting in the right stand at the right time. Beatty continues to enjoy all aspects of deer hunting, and not just hunting for trophy bucks. What surprises Beatty the most about his world record buck is that it still stands after ten years. There are two

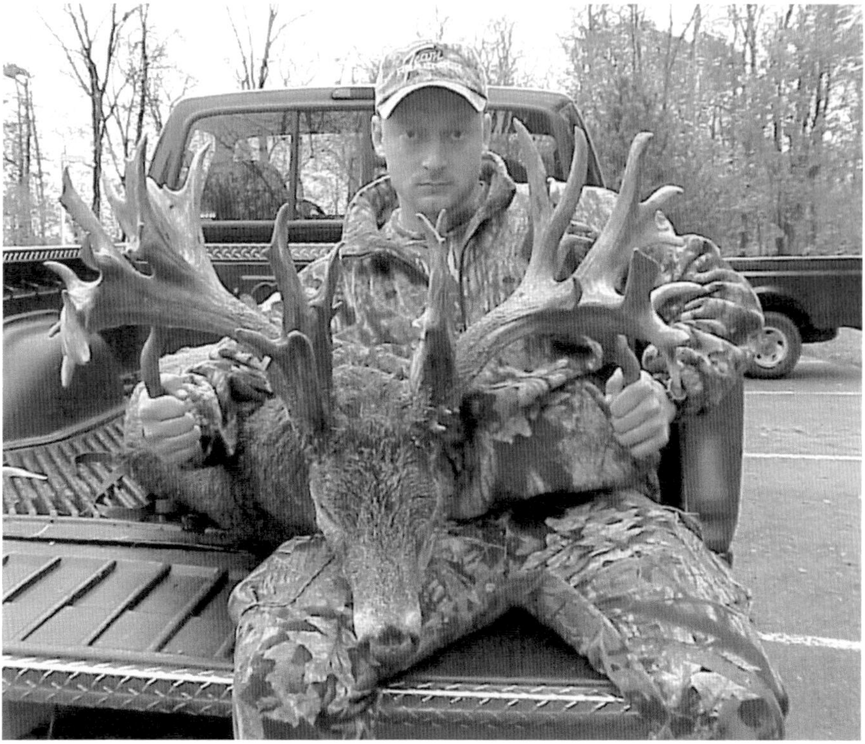

The Beatty Buck may be Ohio's best-known trophy whitetail. The record buck was taken by bowhunter Mike Beatty in Greene County. *Ohio Department of Natural Resources.*

bucks scoring higher than Beatty's (one from Ohio, the Hole-in-the-Horn), but both were found dead along a roadway and a railway.

Beatty's afternoon hunt on November 8 was spent in a tree stand near a cornfield. After spending about an hour with little to no deer activity, Beatty used a doe bleat call to see if he could stir any action. Within ten minutes, a buck approached from Beatty's backside. The buck turned out to be a nice eight-pointer he had seen earlier that summer. The buck was well within range, but too much brush prevented Beatty from releasing an arrow. As he sat in the tree stand, depressed from being denied a shot, Beatty gave a few puffs on his grunt tube and then a few more tries with the doe bleat can. Soon after, Beatty spotted a buck moving his direction through the brushy draw in front of him. He soon realized the buck coming at him was not the eight-pointer but rather a much larger one instead. The wind shifted toward the buck, and Beatty was concerned that the buck would wind him. What the buck did smell was one of several scent bombs that Beatty had released before climbing into his stand. The buck paused within twelve yards, raised his head and curled his lip in response to the luring scent flowing through his nostrils. Beatty released the arrow he had drawn seconds earlier. The arrow hit its mark.

After following a steady blood trail for more than two hundred yards, in the dark, Beatty heard a deer not far in front of him. Reluctantly, Beatty marked his location and retreated to his truck, planning on returning the next day to find his trophy. During the night, heavy rain fell, which drove Beatty nuts thinking that the rain was washing away the blood trail and that the deer would be lost forever. Early the next morning, Beatty and his ten-year-old son were headed to where Beatty had stopped trailing the night before. As the Beattys crested a rise in the field, the young Beatty spotted his dad's buck lying only yards from where the night search had stopped.

The Brad Jerman Buck

On November 10, 2004, Brad Jerman shot a big typical buck that he thought would score pretty high, though he wasn't really sure how high. The buck with matching antlers compiled a score of 201 1/8, which made the Warren County buck the world's largest typical whitetail ever taken with a crossbow and Ohio's typical state record taken with any weapon. Pretty impressive.

On the evening prior, Jerman had planned to shoot some video of the numerous does that regularly visited his deer hunting spot in a brushy field, where he had positioned a tripod stand in the middle of the field. Only small trees existed in the brush land near a suburban area. Does were milling around the field, giving Jerman plenty of video footage. As natural light began to dim, an interesting sight appeared in the viewfinder of his camera. He saw antlers—tall ones. He couldn't believe what he was seeing at first but soon started to grasp the possibility of a huge buck in the area. Jerman waited until complete darkness, and he could still hear the deer close to his tripod stand. No way was he going to chance spooking those deer. When he thought that he could whisper on his cellphone without the deer busting him, he called his wife and informed her of his plan to spend the night in the stand.

A couple hours passed when Jerman decided that he couldn't remain in the stand any longer. He pulled the bolt (arrow) from his crossbow, left them

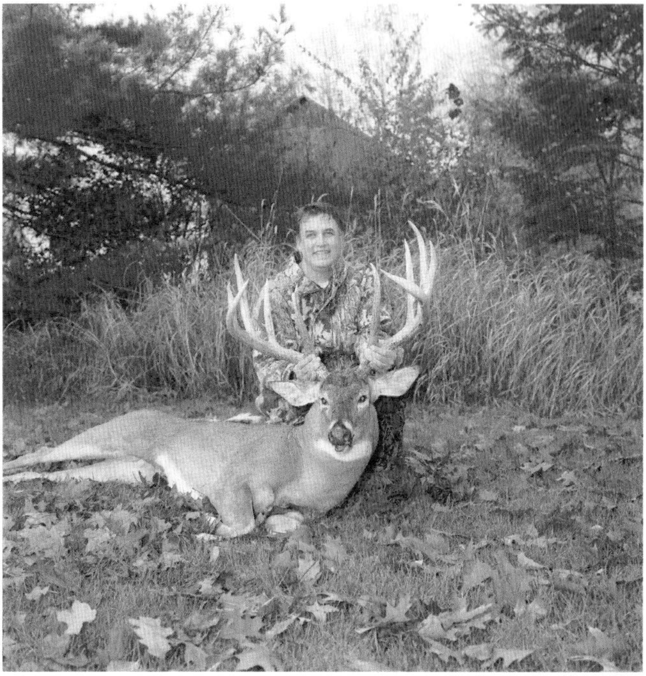

Brad Jerman's record-book buck, taken in 2004 in southwestern Ohio. *Brad Jerman.*

both in the stand and, as quietly as possible, slipped down the ladder. He then belly crawled until he was out of the field and to his truck. Once home, he watched the video on television, which excited him even more about getting back out there. By two o'clock in the morning, Jerman couldn't sleep, so he showered and headed back to try to take the huge buck—if it was still there.

An hour later, he was crawling back to the tripod stand, and when he reached it and stood to climb the ladder, a briar that had stuck to his clothing released, and the sound of this spooked a deer nearby under the cover of extreme darkness. As a reflex, Jerman blew back at the deer that had snorted to alert the other deer of danger. Several times before light began to appear on the horizon, the deer communicated with one another by various snorts and wheezes. At legal shooting light, the does remained in the field and occasionally would cross the several shooting lanes that Jerman had created by mowing. The does were not alone—the big buck was still tending to them. Jerman prepared to take his one shot. As he did, a doe trotted down one of the shooting lanes and past the base of the tripod stand. The buck followed her until he was only six feet from the ladder and stopped to get a smell of a scent dispenser that Jerman had hung earlier. No ethical shot was available, so Jerman had to wait a bit longer.

The buck whirled around and slipped into a thicket at the field's edge. Moments passed, and there was no sign of the buck returning. Another doe walked past the thicket, and the buck pushed his way out toward her and stopped in the shooting lane. Jerman was ready and took the shot. The record breaker ran only twenty-five yards before dropping for the final time. It wasn't until Jerman had a few trophy buck hunters look at the buck that he realized the buck may be something special. And it was.

The Lucky Amish Buck

An Amish hunter harvested an incredible non-typical on opening day of the 2006 archery season. Jonathon Schmucker of Seaman arrowed the thirty-six-pointer during an afternoon hunt in Adams County. The buck

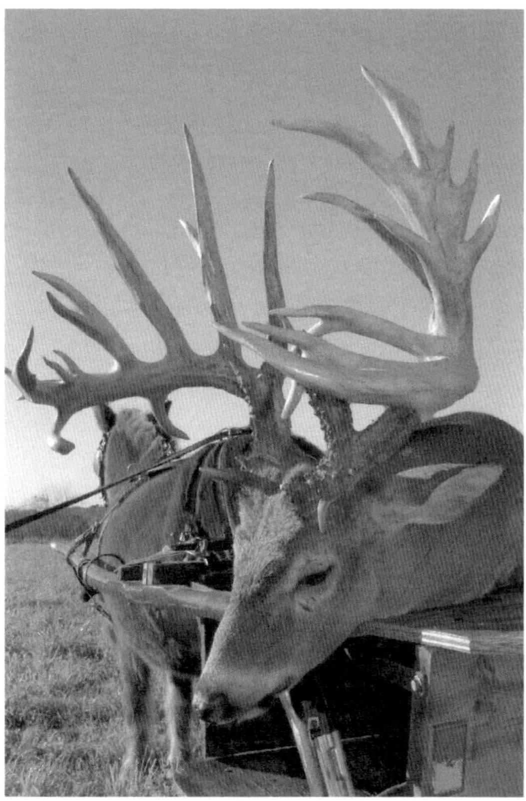

The "Lucky Amish Buck" was harvested in 2006 by Jonathon Schmucker in Adams County. *Tom Cross.*

scored a 291 2/8, which made it the number two whitetail in Ohio and the largest non-typical ever taken with a crossbow in Ohio. Schmucker had been watching the buck for three years and had hunted for the deer each season throughout that time span.

The Old Courthouse Buck

On December 22, 1975, four boys aged eleven to fourteen discovered a dead buck while exploring a woodland in Adams County. The twenty-seven-pointer was frozen in a creek. At the time, it ranked as the second-largest whitetail ever in Ohio. The boys—Donny Swayne, Steve Swayne, Terry Swayne and Tommy Dryden—were on Christmas break from school; little did they know that a gift awaited them in that creek. The boys were on a scouting trip to locate spots to set a few fox traps. They were following a set of fox tracks in the snow when they stumbled upon the buck. Because the buck was frozen in the ice, the boys couldn't pull the buck free. The boys returned home and asked Mrs. Swayne to give them a knife to cut the deer's head off. She reluctantly handed them a dull butcher knife, and they

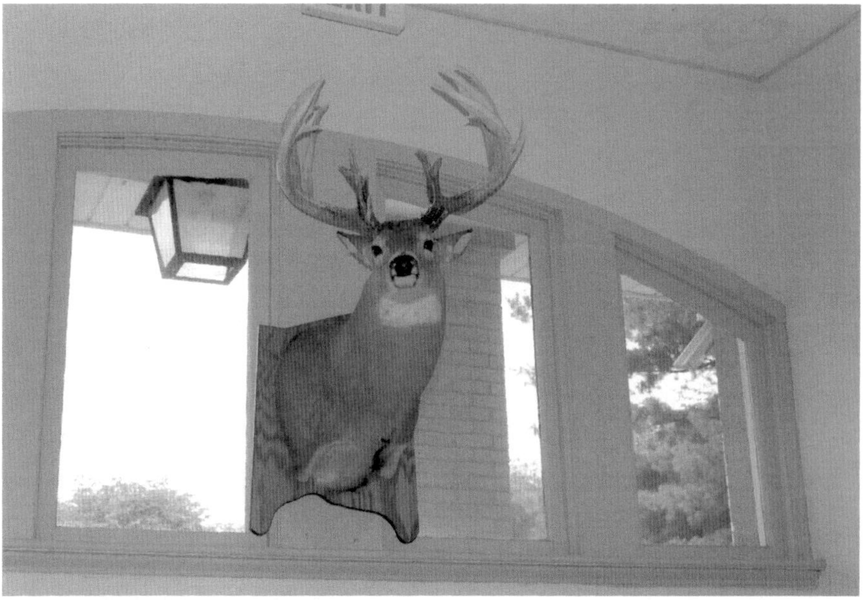

The Old Courthouse Buck hangs in the Adams County Courthouse today. It was found by four boys playing in the woods in 1975. *Robert Loewendick.*

returned to the creek to get their buck. They worked hard at it for some time before the head was finally severed above the shoulders. They returned to the homestead and showed the buck's head to their grandpa. He had never seen a deer like that, he said. After some conflict with wildlife officials, the buck was mounted and returned to Adams County, where it hangs today in the entrance hallway of the county courthouse.

The Hole-in-the-Horn Buck

In 1940, a whitetail buck was found dead near the Ravenna Arsenal in Portage County, which is located in the northeast corner of Ohio. Found lying between a railroad track and a chain link fence, the buck's death was a mystery, but some folks proposed that it was shot. The buck's rack was an immense mass of non-typical antlers. There was a small hole in a drop tine on the right side of the buck's rack, which led speculators to think of the death-by-rifle idea. Years later, during an interview with one of the men who found and retrieved the buck, it was revealed that a piece of wire from the chain link fence was the cause of the hole in the horn. The buck was mounted and placed on the wall of the Kent Canadian Club and hung there for decades. The mount now hangs on a wall at the Ohio Division of Wildlife's District Three office for the public to view.

The buck scored 328 2/8, has forty-five points and a thirty-three-inch spread. The Hole-in-the-Horn buck is the number two non-typical of all time.

The Stephens Buck

The story of this buck shows how quick a new record can be set and lost in just a few months. Well, not all of the record anyway. Let me explain.

On November 30, 2009, Brian Stephens shot an eighteen-point non-typical with a muzzleloader in Highland County. The official score was 232 5/8. Impressive for sure, but the most remarkable element about this buck's antlers are the length of the main beams. The buck's main beams measurements are 35⅛ inches and 34⅛ inches—the longest main beams ever recorded in the world.

Four days after Stephens had the final scoring completed on his buck, the owner of another Highland County muzzleloader-killed deer came forward

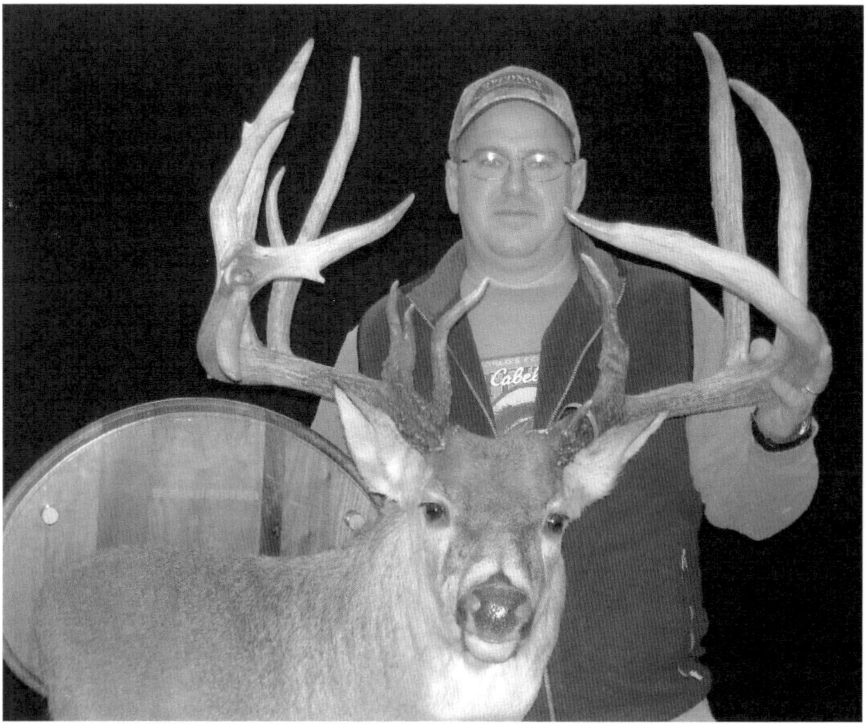

Brian Stephens's trophy was taken in Highland County in 2009. *Ohio Department of Natural Resources.*

to have his buck rescored. Tom Luschek killed the challenging buck in 1993. He had the deer officially scored at an outdoor show in 1994 but never had the score recorded. Luschek's buck scored 237 4/8. Brian Stephens's buck moved to Ohio's second overall muzzleloader non-typical kill, but the extraordinarily long main beams remain world records today.

THE BUCKEYE BIG BUCK CLUB

The Buckeye Big Buck Club is Ohio's official record keeping club and was created in 1958 to bring attention and appreciation to Ohio's trophy whitetails. From the BBBC's website, the club's intentions are as follows: "To increase the appreciation of Ohio's white-tailed deer herd, which due to a comprehensive and successful management program of the Division

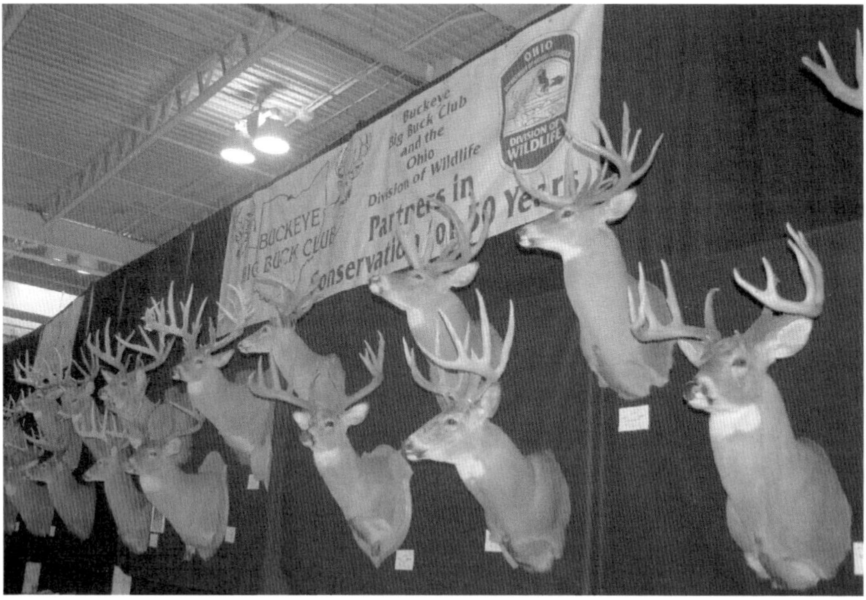

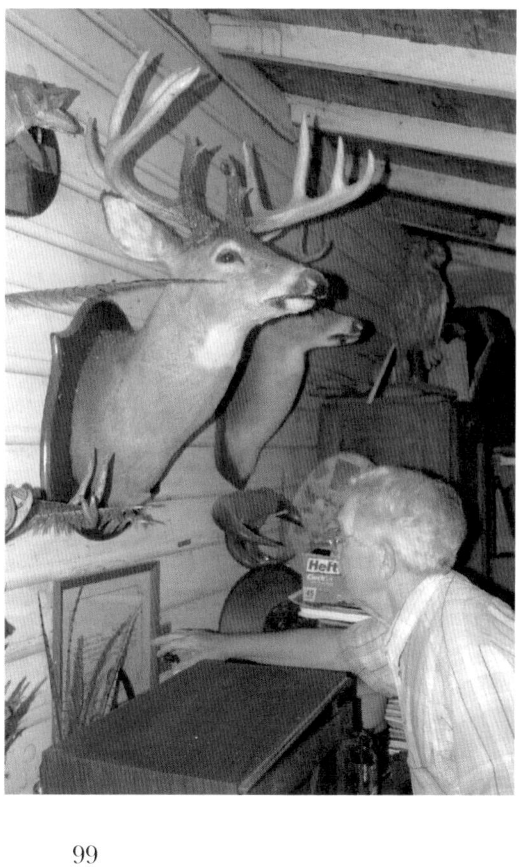

Above: The Buckeye Big Buck Club has scored and recognized the deer and the deer hunter for more than fifty years. *Robert Loewendick.*

Right: Karl Wilburn and his Buckeye Big Buck Club buck, taken in the 1980s. *Robert Loewendick.*

of Wildlife, and improved habitat, is now at a record high level." The club's goals are to encourage trophy hunting by Ohio hunters, establish and maintain a permanent record of Ohio's trophy deer taken in fair chase, foster wise management of this valuable resource and promote a positive relationship among hunter and landowners. Each year, the club honors hunters who harvest "typical" deer that meet the minimum 140-inch scoring requirement and "non-typical" deer meeting a minimum 160-inch score requirement. Scores are determined by a series of measurements using the Boone & Crockett scoring system. The BBBC record book has more than seventeen thousand entries.

Chapter 8

WILD TALES

Possibly one of the most entertaining products of deer hunting is the stories that come from the adventures. Some stories are believable and true. Some are unbelievable and true. Others are believable and unbelievable and are nothing more than bogus tales. Either way, they are entertaining. This chapter holds a sampling of several Ohio deer hunting stories I have gathered. Some have the source noted and some not. These stories either appeared in old newspapers or have been passed on from hunter to hunter through several generations. While visiting little country stores during deer hunting seasons, a person can come away with a pile of tales in a short time. Some of the authors of these stories withheld their names for several reasons, but the stories are still worth telling. Some of these tales are recent, and some are from decades ago. Maybe you have experienced something similar to what you are about to read, or maybe you know someone who has. One thing is for sure. If a person spends multiple days pursuing deer across Ohio's diverse geography, they will experience a few moments worthy of being retold.

Gone to the Dogs

This story is from the book *The Ohio Hunter*, written by James Nagel and Richard Helwig, published in 1866 and reprinted in *Farmland News*. The story is from the accounts of Samuel E. Edwards, a pioneer who lived in northeast Ohio.

In the fall of 1838, I commenced a series of hunting excursions which proved very successful and it is my intention now to give the reader a detail of some of the adventures that followed. I commenced in October and that autumn and the following winter I killed 38 deer. One of my first successes was on the Sabbath. I had only my gun and knife, no dog, and after several hours in the woods I came across an old buck that I succeeded in wounding. The artful deer was too experienced to be shot again. I followed him five miles, close to where there lived Mr. H., a devoted Methodist. In those days, I paid not attention to days myself and did not regard other people's preferences very highly. I told the gentleman that I had wounded a large buck and asked him to bring his dog and help me trail him. When I first addressed him, he said, "Heigh!" Bad luck will follow you for hunting on the Sabbath. But upon it being stipulated that I promise him half of the spoils, he consented and went along. I told him that the buck was a very large one and that I was afraid it would hurt his dog.

He replied that there was no danger, that no deer that ran in these woods could hurt his dog. Well, I decided that if he was willing to risk losing his dog, then I was willing to risk losing the deer. We proceeded along together until we came in sight of the deer. He told his dog to go, and away the dog went. The poor deer was weak from loss of blood and could not do much running. When he saw that he was likely to be overtaken by the dog, the deer turned and commenced a different kind of warfare. The dog, like his master, was very brave and made no halt and met the deer, not exactly face to face, but head to head. The head of the deer being a little harder, the poor dog was soon howling piteously.

I was willing to see a little fun and told Mr. H. to go and help his dog. He ran up with a little branch in his hand and demanded that the deer let his dog alone. The deer obeyed that injunction and instead took after Mr. H., who proved himself to be a very fine pedestrian, but hardy equal to occasion. However, before the deer was able to do him any serious injury, he found himself pursued in the rear. The buck was thrown and I caught him by the horns and told Mr. H. to cut his throat. Mr. H. walked up to him just as he lay perfectly still and have his throat cut without resistance. He drew up his legs and kicked and sent Mr. H. rolling down the hill, making very graceful revolutions as he went. The infuriated buck made several more jumps, carrying me along as an appendage to his horns. But after a little time, with the help of the dog, I succeeded in bringing him again to the ground.

I called for Mr. H. to come again and cut his throat, but now he said he would not because it was Sunday and he did not believe it was good luck to hunt on Sunday. I at last succeeded in accomplishing the difficult throat cutting alone. We then divided the deer between us and each started for home just as the shades of night came on. The weight I had to carry was 80 pounds and the distance to be traveled was over five miles. Folks, that's a pretty impressive hunting experience. I've talked with lots of deer hunters in my life but I have yet to meet one who had to bulldog a wounded animal and slit its throat. And then, after all that, carried 80 pounds of meat five miles through the woods to get home. I'm thinking that the Ohio frontier might have been too tough for me. I'd have probably wound up trying to live on roots and berries.

A Second Story from *The Ohio Hunter*

To be a successful hunter in northwestern Ohio, a man like Samuel Edwards needed a lot of courage, a trusty rifle like Old Killall, a hunting knife, a tomahawk and at least one good dog. Young Edwards soon learned the value of the latter when he acquired and trained Bravo. Not long after my deer hunt with the Methodist, I went out and wounded another deer. I had no dog yet, so I had to follow it until it lay down behind a log. I went very close to it and was taking aim at his head when suddenly he sprang toward me. I found refuge behind a small tree. He jumped against the tree with his head and I thus caught him by his horns. I was now in quite a dilemma. It required all my strength and both of my hands to hold him there, so I had to devise some expedient for cutting his throat. After he stopped rearing and plunging, I managed to hold one of his horns with my foot and the other with my hand. With my free hand I got out my knife and slit his throat. Just as I had finished my work I heard a loud laugh and, looking around, I saw some old hunters who had concealed themselves to watch the sport. They came out of their hiding place and congratulated me on my success.

But I have had many more difficult encounters since that one and I am not dead yet. Soon after this I bought me a dog, named him Bravo and trained him especially for hunting. He would stay close by my side, no matter if he saw 20 deer, until I told him to chase them. Then he was sure to humble even the proudest deer. On one occasion, I wounded one in the foot. It was a cold day and the ice was frozen about half an inch thick. The deer started across the ice and broke through. He waded on, breaking the ice as he went. Bravo followed him and the deer managed to get him under the ice. As soon as I discovered the condition of my dog, I waded into the water up to my knees and rescued my favorite from drowning. He was large and shaggy and he was soon ornamented with a row of icicles hanging all around his great body. I relieved him of these with my knife. I had got my gun wet while rescuing the dog, so I could not shoot. And there now remained no means of capture but the chase.

I gave Bravo the word and he was soon bounding away rapidly in the direction of the deer. I followed after him. And if Bravo had not cornered his prey, I think I should have been a long time overtaking them. But I soon knew by the barking that he had his enemy in close quarters. When I came upon them, Bravo was standing at a distance, barking. But he did not seem anxious for a closer intimacy until there was someone to share the sport with him. Upon discovering my dog's embarrassing situation, I immediately threw aside my gun and shot pouch and, with tomahawk in hand, proceeded to the contest.

I first struck the deer on the horns, but the blow glanced off and my tomahawk flew far out of my hand. The deer was about to give me a toss with his horns when I disappointed his plans by placing a firm grasp about those convenient members and holding him at a respectful distance. Bravo caught him by the hind leg and held him firmly. Then, between us both, we laid the dexterous animal on the ground. But there was nothing accessible to cut his throat with. I had left my butcher knife in my shot pouch and my tomahawk was lost. So I ordered Bravo to bite his throat. But the deer was not of a mind to submit to such a tedious process of dying. By means of all the floundering and jumping about, I at last came upon my lost tomahawk, at which time I considerably expedited the process.

Playing Dead

Sandusky County, 1970s. The hunter had seen the buck he shot at earlier in the day and was working his way closer for a better shot. The buck was busy chomping on acorns, and the hunter went undetected as he approached. The shot was a good one, and the buck fell where it stood. The hunter tied on his

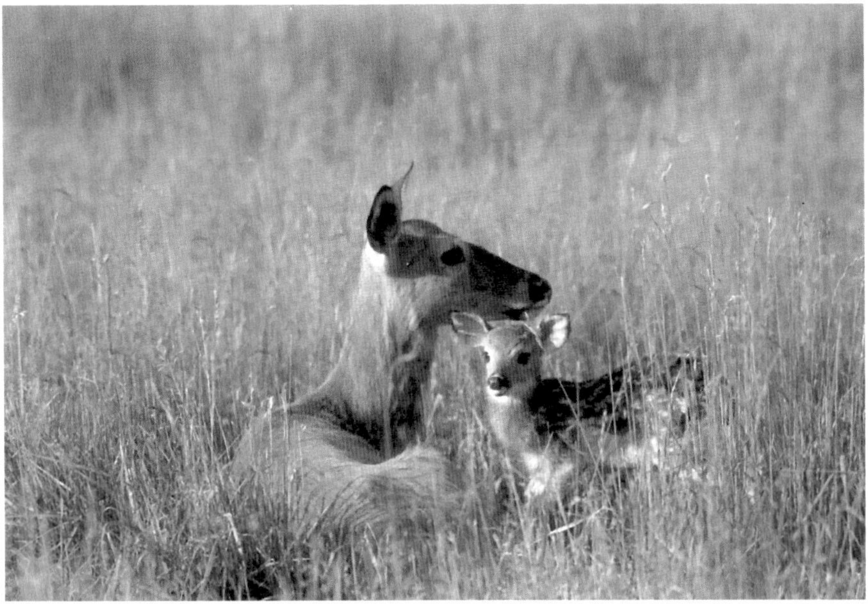

Many wild tales begin small and grow big if nurtured along, as this fawn will. But some stories are huge from the start. *Judy Wells.*

deer tag and was about to field-dress the buck when he realized that he had left his knife in the car. He wasn't concerned about someone coming along and taking his deer because he hadn't seen another hunter for two days.

The hunter made the trek to his car and retrieved his knife and a short piece of rope to attach to the antlers to pull it back. As he neared the spot where he left the buck, he couldn't see it lying there. He paused to look around to make sure that he hadn't made a wrong turn. He located the tree he was leaning against when he took the shot. He was in the right place, but where in the heck was his buck? He searched along and under the creek bank near where the buck fell, thinking that it may have revived enough and kicked its way down there. It wasn't. He walked the woods a hundred yards in each direction before finding a small speck of blood on a leaf several yards from where the deer had fallen. He finally gave up and went to town. He told several friends about what happened, and they teased him about the deer taking his tag with it when it escaped.

Two weeks later, a friend pulled into his driveway. To the hunter's surprise, his friend had his bloody deer tag in his hand. He asked him how he got his hands on the tag. The friend informed him that the buck was hit by a car the night before and that the guy who was moving the buck off to the side of the road noticed the tag still attached to the antler. The buck was a mess from the run in with the car, so the man left the deer but took the tag and dropped it off at the nearest deer checking station. The store owner gave the tag to the friend to deliver the tag to its rightful owner. The buck was killed over three miles from where he was temporarily slowed by the hunter's slug.

TWO FOR ONE

Ross County, 1980s. Nine deer were feeding in a bean field as a group. Two bucks were among the group, and one of them was what the hunter was looking for. It was a typical antlered buck and heavy in body. Although the deer were well out of range, they were close enough for the hunter to see which one he wanted to take a shot at. The field edge was too dry to attempt a stalk, so the hunter waited for a few minutes longer to see what the deer were going to do. Darkness was coming, and the hunter knew that he had to make a move or wait until tomorrow.

He was confident that there were no other hunters in the woodlot behind the deer, so he decided that he would try a long-range shot and see what happened. One buck was on the left, and the other was in the middle of the group. The one in the middle was the bigger of the two. The hunter pointed his shotgun and adjusted the end of the barrel for the long-distance shot. The hunter pulled the gun down and considered if he should take such a risky shot. He talked himself into it.

After the shot was fired, the deer scattered and retreated into the woods. The hunter could see that a deer was down, and the excitement was released. He began the walk to have a look at his deer. While walking, he thought about how the long shot turned out to be a killing one. He had shot one deer in the past as it was running and dropped it. He began to consider himself a pretty good shot and couldn't wait to see where exactly the slug had hit the deer. Some of his hunting buddies often told him that he took shots he shouldn't take, but with another deer down, maybe they should take some lessons from him.

As he closed in within fifty yards of the downed buck, he couldn't believe how big the body was. It appeared to be twice the size of an average-sized deer. A few yards closer, and it became clear what he was truly looking at. Lying on the opposite side of the buck was a small doe. The hunter's slug had passed through the buck's back, severing nerves along the spine, and continued on into the little doe standing behind the buck. Two dead deer, one slug, one deer tag and one hunter who learned the lesson not to take ridiculously long shots and be absolutely sure of your target and beyond.

Broad Head

Greene County, 1980s, from Karl Wilburn. Karl was sitting in a tree stand along a fence row when one of several good bucks walked beneath him. The deer milled around for several minutes before Karl was offered a shot. He released his arrow cleanly, but it went off its intended path, and the broadhead hit the deer in the head. To Karl, it sounded like two pieces of lumber being smacked together. The buck ran a short distance and out of sight. Karl could hear the buck slashing around in the brush, trying to dislodge the arrow sticking out of the side of its head. After a few moments

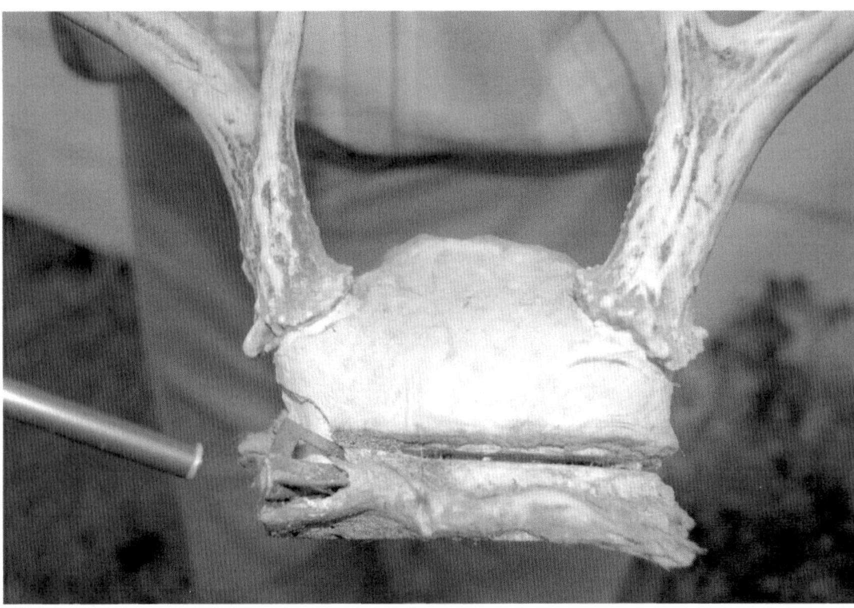

An arrowhead lodged in a deer skull. *Robert Loewendick.*

of trying, the buck broke off the arrow and ran off out of Karl's sight and hearing. Karl searched for the buck but never found it dead.

While observing a buck in a field that Karl had been hunting religiously, a smaller buck entered the field alongside a larger buck. When Karl focused his binoculars on the smaller buck, he soon realized that it was the buck he had shot in the head. The buck had a patch of dried blood on the side of its face, confirming Karl's assumption. Before Karl could put together a plan to stalk the buck to finish what he started, the buck went out of sight chasing a doe.

The following spring, Karl was telling a friend about the buck and the arrow being broken off and the broadhead likely remaining in the buck's skull. The friend looked surprised and told Karl he needed to share his story with a man they both new. The friend thought that the man might have an answer to Karl's broadhead-in-the-head deer mystery. So he did and the mystery was solved.

A week or so after Karl last saw the buck during the fall archery season, the man found a torn-up area several yards in diameter in the middle of a field. The area was the site of a buck battle, and lying in the middle of the circle was a dead buck that had succumbed to wounds from the fight. The man retrieved a saw and returned to cut off the antlers. As soon as he began cutting, he discovered the broadhead lodged in the skull. Knowing that the buck's story would likely come about someday, the man kept the skull cap with the broadhead firmly in place.

SECRETS AND SHED ANTLERS

Adams County. Two brothers and avid deer hunters were often amused by a few other deer hunters who went to all lengths to keep their deer hunting a secret. The secretive hunters would sit at the local restaurant and not share any deer hunting tales with fellow hunters also eating there. They seemed to want to keep their hunting lands a secret and keep the deer living there a mystery to others. The secretive hunters assumed that their secret was safe, and in their minds, everyone wanted to know where they were hunting.

One day, after arriving at the restaurant, the two brothers thought that they would have some fun. One of the brothers had killed a buck that morning and had the deer strapped to the vehicle. The secretive hunters asked where the boy shot the deer, and in response, the boy announced loudly the exact location, including road name and property owner. The secretive hunters nearly choked on their food, as what the boy said revealed the secret hunting grounds. The boys didn't actually get their deer there, but they surely enjoyed seeing the two mysterious hunters get the news that their secret was not such a secret.

The same two brothers would continue the fun by situating a large set of shed antlers half sticking up out of their truck bed when arriving at the local deer checking station. Arriving and departing deer hunters would hurry over to the boys' truck to see the massive deer that was supporting the huge antlers rising above the truck bed. The only thing the hunters would see were two boys laughing and shaking their heads as they walked into the store.

Pull Your Pants Up

Morgan County, 1970s. The young boy would wake early with his father and watch him prepare for a day of deer hunting. The boy asked questions about this and why father needed that. He asked questions about what to do in various deer hunting situations. And, of course, he often asked to go deer hunting with his father more than once. His father always answered that when he thought the boy was ready he would let him know. The boy always hoped that the next season would be the one when he would get the invite to go.

The boy hounded his father for weeks preceding the opening of deer season to let him come along. The father finally agreed to his joining him as long as the boy practiced sitting quietly and holding completely still. For two weeks, the boy practiced several times each day. One Sunday afternoon, the boy asked his father to join him on the porch. His father could read the newspaper, and the boy would sit in the corner of the porch perfectly quiet and stone still, so he could prove that he was ready for deer hunting. His father was impressed and then informed him that it was time to practice gun safety and shooting skills. The boy excitedly accepted the offer. The boy's marksmanship was impressive from the first shot. A couple lessons of walking through high weeds and through the woods with a shotgun and the boy was ready to hunt.

The boy couldn't sleep the night before his first hunt. When his father woke, the boy was already eating breakfast at the table. They discussed

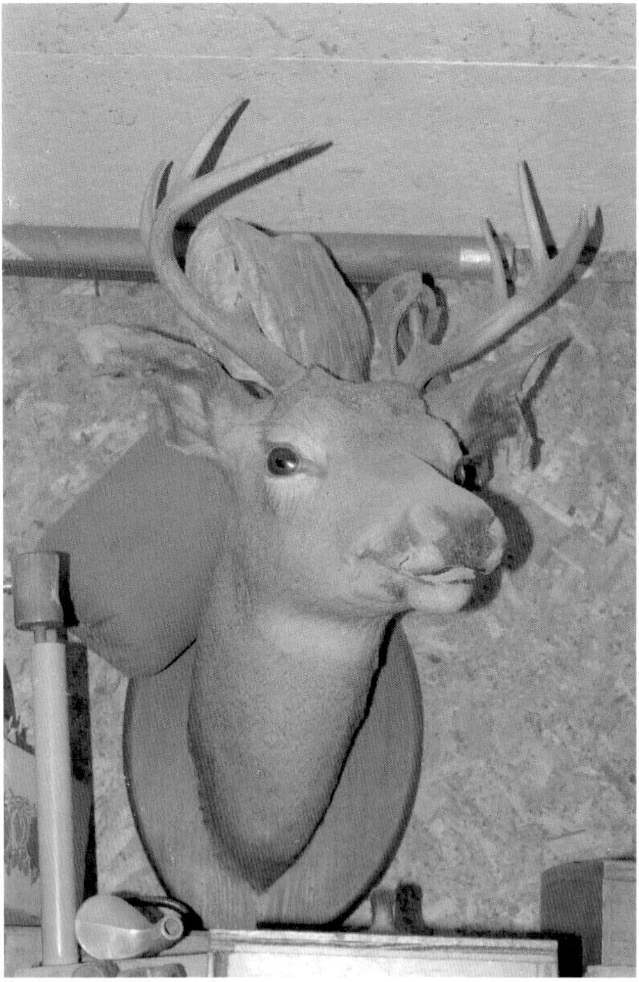

Often, old deer mounts come with wild tales attached. *Robert Loewendick.*

which tree stand which of them would hunt from and a couple other details before leaving. The father told the boy to go to the bathroom one more time before they left the house, but the boy said that he was fine and pushed his father toward the door.

The sun had been up for an hour when a string of does came past the father's tree stand. What excited the father the most was that the deer were heading straight toward his son's location. He let the deer pass without taking a shot so as not disrupt his son's opportunity to take his first deer. The father and son were not far apart, only forty yards at most, but the father couldn't see his son clearly. The deer continued on in the direction of his son, and the father was anticipating a shotgun blast at any moment. Several more minutes passed and no shot was heard.

An hour had passed, and the father was gazing at his son's position to see if there was something wrong. The father couldn't stand it any longer so he descended his tree stand and headed for his son. When he arrived under his son's stand, he saw that the boy was fine except for a look of depression covering his face. The father asked him if he was okay, and the boy nodded his head in agreement. When the boy was asked if he saw the deer come his way, he answered yes again. His father asked him if he had a shot, and the boy said yes he did. Now the father was a bit irritated and asked why the boy let the deer pass.

The boy was sitting in his stand when he got the urge to relieve himself shortly before the deer arrived. He quietly snuck down the ladder, crept a few yards behind his stand location, lowered his pants and let nature happen. While he was sitting over a small log, with his pants piled around his ankles, he heard something coming. He watched the deer parade past his stand, which was where he left his shotgun as a safety measure. He couldn't do anything but simply sit there and watch the deer slowly walk on by. One doe did stop for a few seconds, put her nose in the air and then hustled on.

After hearing this, the father had to sit down because he was laughing so hard. The boy didn't crack a smile for weeks after.

I See You

Licking County, 1990s. The deer hunter was finally granted permission to hunt a property that was known for holding big bucks. He was excited to get some scouting done, so he began talking with some of the residents who lived in the small subdivision next to the open fields and brushy woodlots that he was about to hunt. A few of the residents told him about several deer they frequently saw feeding in the fields morning and night. He added this information to other scouting notes he was compiling and put together a plan.

He chose to put a tree stand in a maple tree within sight of the subdivision but close to an acre of unmowed brush. As he sat in the tree stand during the second day of hunting the property, he remembered one of the residents telling him that there was one buck that always kept to himself and would appear in different sections of the property on different days. He didn't seem to follow a pattern. The hunter assured the resident that he would be able to figure the deer out. The resident told the hunter that she had watched these deer for years and that they seemed to be pretty smart, but he was the hunter and she wished him luck.

For two weeks, the hunter hunted the property, skipping a day or two in between hunts to keep the deer unsuspecting. The days he did hunt, he would see a few does and a couple small bucks but never the big buck he had seen with binoculars once and heard about several times. More weeks went by with the same results. The season ended without any deer being taken from the property. In his disgust, the hunter pulled the tree stand and was loading it in his truck when he saw a woman walking across the field from the subdivision.

He remembered her being the person who told him about the big ol' buck that he never saw. She told him that she wanted to show him something, and she pulled out an envelope of photos from her coat pocket. The photos were taken by her and her camera with a fine zoom lens. The photos made the hunter's jaw drop. The photos held images of the hunter walking to his tree stand in the afternoon. She wasn't stalking him, but her photos did reveal a sly being. In the background of the photo of the hunter walking with his bow in hand was a dark image of a buck's silhouette. Several afternoons, when the lady was home, she would glass the field with her camera on a tripod out the window of her living room. More than once she spotted, after looking very closely, the old buck tucked into a brush pile only thirty yards from the hunter's tree stand. The buck watched him come and go. And once the hunter's truck started to leave the parking spot, the buck would raise, shake, stretch and then calmly enter the field to feed.

THE SHOT

Harrison County, 1960s. The boy and his grandfather were slowly working their way down a steep ridge. Both hunters were carrying shotguns, the boy a twenty-gauge and his grandfather a twelve-gauge. The hunters took a break when they reached the creek to have a snack and check their guns. They sat talking about the two bucks they jumped earlier that morning, and they were disappointed they didn't get a shot off. The boy was telling his grandfather

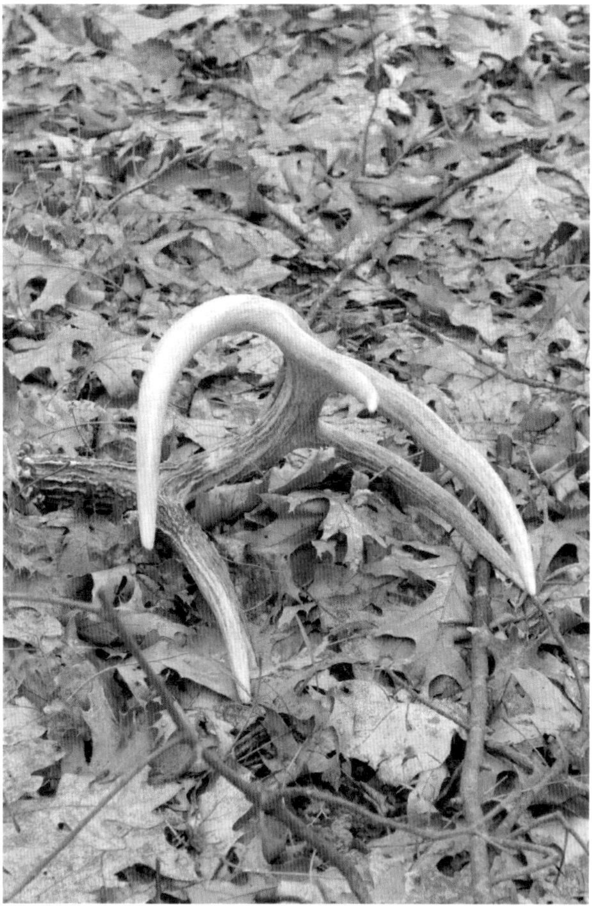

Deer legends don't always have a body to support them, but only a clue or two can keep the legend alive. *Robert Loewendick.*

what he thought they should do next (and was hoping to get his first deer) when a doe appeared on the side of the hill behind the boy. The grandfather winked at the fourteen-year-old and whispered to him to be quiet. The doe was staring in their direction but wasn't sure of what she was seeing. Another deer appeared next to her, and then a buck soon walked past both of them to have a look.

The hunters remained still, but the boy was about to explode if he didn't turn around soon and see what his grandfather was seeing. The deer began to relax as the wind shifted enough to carry the hunters' scent away from the deer. The buck went to feeding and the does joined him. The grandfather nodded his head toward the boy's gun, and the boy slowly reached for it. The deer were still not aware of the hunters' presence and were working their way around the hillside. When the grandfather saw that the deer were somewhat out of sight because of a few trees between them and the hunters, he pulled the boy's shoulder around to line his grandson up for a shot when the deer cleared the trees. The boy slipped off his gun's safety and waited.

The buck was the first to reappear. The boy fired his shotgun, and the buck whirled and jumped into a bounding run. The boy shot again. The deer kept going. He shot his last slug from his twenty-gauge and the deer fell. The entire episode lasted only a few seconds, and things were a blur in the boy's mind. He turned to his grandfather, who was behind him, crouching on one knee with his twelve-gauge resting on his other knee. The two hunters stood and hugged each other after they saw the buck was lying there motionless. The boy yelled out that he had finally got a buck. His first deer ever. His grandfather told him that there would be a celebration tonight and that the boy's buck was on the menu.

The boy's father met them at the grandfather's place to help butcher the buck. A few photos were taken, and the story was shared among visiting cousins and friends. The boy and his buck's admirers continued their conversation outside of the barn and left the processing chore to his dad and grandfather. As the father was cutting the hide from the carcass, he said to his father that he was surprised at the damage the little twenty-gauge slug did to the flesh surrounding the killing wound. The grandfather agreed and kept working. The father was cutting some meat away and found the slug. It was evident that the slug was not from a twenty-gauge but rather from a twelve-gauge instead. The grandfather asked his son to hand him the slug and told him to not say a word to his grandson.

Five years later, the grandfather passed away. That same year, during an afternoon hunt being shared by the son and father, the father informed his son of the truth behind this story. His son smiled and looked up to the sky. He looked back at his dad with moist eyes and told his dad that the deer would always be his and grandpa's.

Chapter 9

PASSING ON OHIO'S DEER HUNTING LEGACY

Watching my son's eyes scanning the open forestland surrounding us was a joy. As early evening began to fall, the deer were expected to be following the forest trail to the open field not far away to begin their nightly feeding. Rob had hunted deer with me before on occasion, but this day was the first day of Ohio's two-day youth season, and the twelve-year-old was the hunter and I the observer.

Rob whispered the occasional question about this or that, things that he was seeing around him. That natural world always provides more entertainment to youth than a kid can absorb in one sitting. Even while deer hunting, the wonders of the natural world continue to provide a show. Squirrels were leaping from tree to tree, hustling mouthfuls of nuts for winter storage. When a squirrel would slip and make an acrobatic save, Rob would turn his head slightly to make eye contact with me and smile.

Deeper into the woods, I heard movement. Although I didn't see any movement, I was certain that it was a whitetail. The place was right and so was the time. A moment later, I saw deer legs moving, and soon after the entire doe was in sight, with two others following in line. I turned my eyes to confirm if Rob was seeing what I was, and his attention was still on the working squirrels. I continued to switch my stare from the deer to Rob and back to the other again. When Rob spotted the deer walking our way, his eyes opened wide like a blooming flower. I had to put my hand on his leg to remind him to hold still. He did.

Rob's deer hunt this day reminded me of the day I took my first deer. It was a day I had a prize to take home for my participation in Ohio's esteemed deer hunting heritage, and my father, too, was present to celebrate the day. Hunting in the Loewendick family was considered a treasured pastime as it was with thousands of Ohioan families and individuals. Having the opportunity to pursue one of the nation's greatest big game animals was a privilege not taken for granted by most. Ohio had gone from a state that had no deer to a state harboring more than 600,000 deer eighty years later. The white-tailed deer was a prized element to be seen in the Ohio landscape once again.

The deer had followed the script perfectly. The lead doe hesitated before descending the small slope to cross the creek when Rob fired the shotgun that once belonged to his grandfather. The doe fell instantly. I checked to make sure that Rob had put the gun safety back on, and he had; then I hugged him. I was more proud of him than he was of himself. He was still shaking some but smiling from ear to ear just the same. We watched the other two deer depart, and then we went to retrieve the boy's first deer. Rob knelt beside her and stroked her back as if a long-lost pet had been returned. We talked for a few moments about how Rob felt about taking the doe. He was excited to have accomplished what he set out to do but, at the same time, felt some remorse for taking the deer's life. I was glad to see the mixed reaction coming from my son. It confirmed to me that he had retained the themes from numerous discussions about hunting in preparation for that day. As he struggled to drag the doe through the woods to our home, he would pause every twenty yards and admire her. As a father and as his hunting mentor, I couldn't have been more proud. The proverbial hunting torch that was handed to me by my father was now in the hands of the next generation. And as a conservationist, a most important goal was reached; Ohio's deer and those who admire them are also winners.

Generations of hunters across Ohio have been blessed with quality deer hunting close to home or at least within a short drive. Our culture today may not resemble our ways one hundred years ago in the general public. But for those who have been a part of Ohio's deer hunting heritage, from the 1940s up to present times, the traditions are nearly the same as they have always been. For most deer hunters, the time spent outdoors is not just about hunting deer. Spending quality time with family and friends creates a pool from which to draw in later years. Most deer hunting stories start with the names and/or relationships of the people who were along for or a part

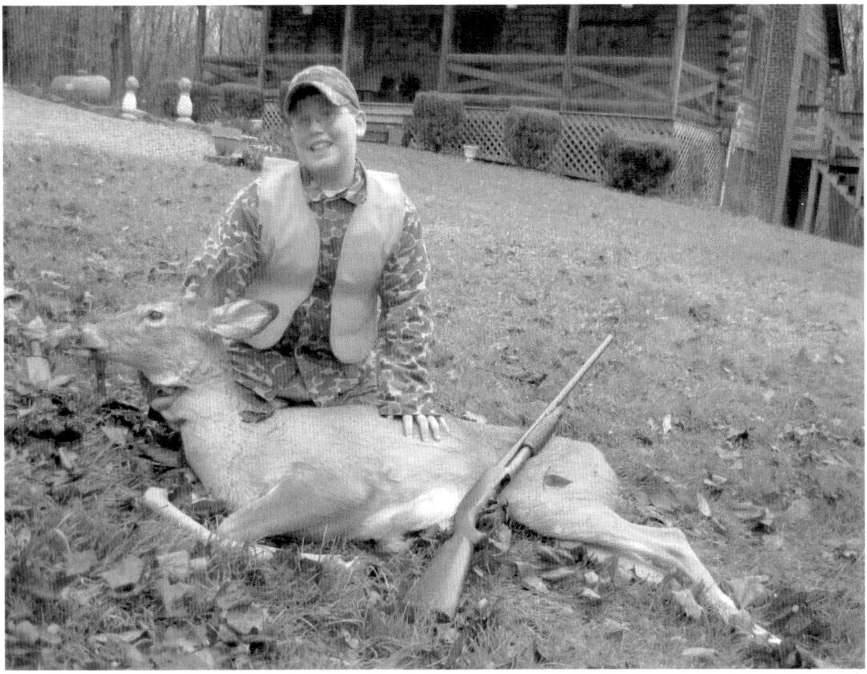

The author's son, Robbie, with his first Ohio whitetail, taken with his grandfather's shotgun. *Robert Loewendick.*

of the hunt. Deer hunting has several valuable components, and the deer is only one of them.

As a young boy, it was a treat to be able to tag along with my older brother and our cousins, most of whom were older than I, on any hunting excursion of any size or at any place. When I reached my teen years, I began to take my place in the family's hunting circle. Of course, I became the "dog" when it came time for deer drives and such, but I never complained too much for fear of not being able to join future hunts. Once in my twenties, I had nephews and younger cousins join the hunting portion of the clan, and they became the dogs. By that time, though, I was approaching deer hunting more so as an individual event by spending more time sitting in tree stands, stalking and still hunting for deer. Even then, though, I would join a family member or two and possibly a couple buddies for an early morning or late afternoon deer hunt. One thing was always clear: the camaraderie gained from hunting together was intact every day thereafter and at all times—hunting or not hunting.

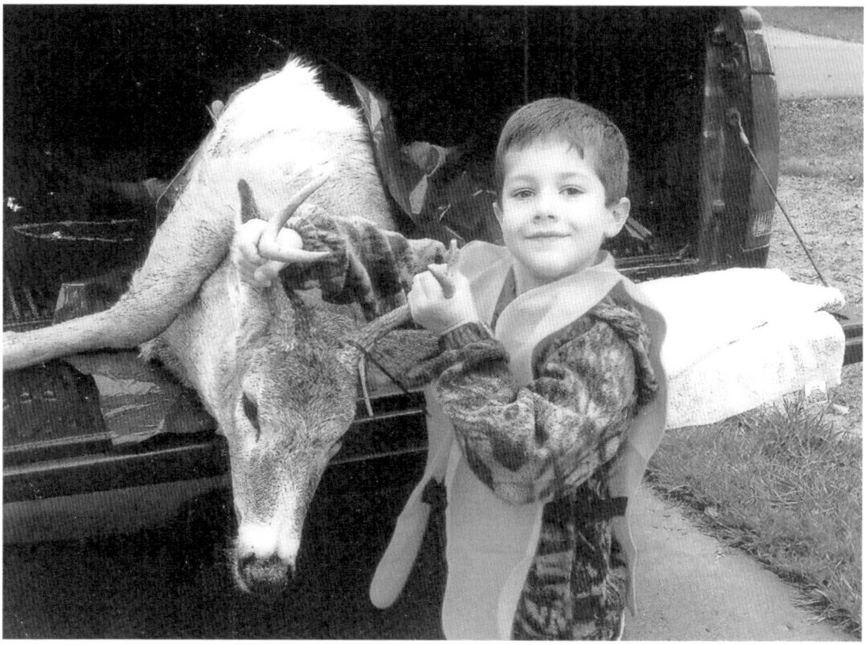

Six-year-old Brayden Beardsley is a third-generation hunter. The hunting heritage runs deep throughout Ohio. *Beardsley.*

Soon after deer and deer hunting seasons returned to Ohio, kids began to experience new thrills and lessons in the forests and fields. Following in the footsteps of their older relatives, new members were created in the deer hunting community. Today, youth have a plethora of activities to gobble up their time at a very young age, and hunting, or any pursuit in the outdoors not including a ball, is often at the bottom of that list. Multiple programs have been initiated to combat the disconnection of youth from the outdoor world and are having some success. When my daughter was very young, I would take her for walks in the woods to explore and ensure that she had a firm grasp on the importance of the natural world. She went along on a few hunts in her early teen years and even shot a squirrel of her own during one of those hunts. She is in her twenties now and still spends a decent amount of time recreating with nature, not so much with hunting but enjoying nature just the same.

Designated youth-only deer seasons have proved successful through the last decade. These special seasons allow the hunting mentor to focus solely on the young hunter and ensure that all safety and ethical procedures are followed. A positive time in the outdoors will increase the odds of a young person returning to the woods and waters for the remainder of their lives. And hopefully they will pass on the enthusiasm to other young ones along the way. Conservation organizations, both national and regional, provide youth events throughout the year, and Ohio clubs have often been recognized for their efforts. The events provide opportunities for kids to try archery, shooting and fishing and to learn about other conservational tools. It also teaches them to appreciate doing those things with others, which starts building the camaraderie factor early in their lives.

The Four Stages of Being a Hunter

Several years ago, an old man told me that there are four stages of a hunter's hunting career. Now at the age of forty-five, I've discovered that the old man was correct. Each stage comes at different times for different hunters, and some hunters get stuck in a particular stage and never evolve. But for a hunter to have a healthy outlook and appreciation on hunting and on life in general, the fourth stage is considered the place to be.

During the first stage, a hunter wants to get their first kill and in a hurry. Doesn't matter really how big or impressive the quarry, just the fact that they went hunting and brought home a kill.

During the second stage, the hunter's goal is to limit each time they go out. If the zone they are hunting allows six deer to be taken, then they won't rest or consider their season a total success until six deer have been killed.

During stage three, the tide turns from quantity to quality. A hunter in stage three wants to bag the biggest buck in the county or, even better, the state. It's common for deer hunters to linger in stage three for many seasons. Stage three is an extremely populated stage. That doesn't include the young boy who dreams about shooting a trophy buck to hang alongside his father's in the family room or the average deer hunter who appreciates the possibility of a mature buck appearing under his stand and providing a shot; that's just a human trait. Stage three is where most of the money spent on deer hunting gear and accessories is made. The quest for a trophy buck can get expensive in both time and financial measurements.

Stage four is reached when a hunter can get up early, or not so early, and casually enter the woods without much urgency. A stage four hunter is more aware of his surroundings and appreciates each step and each breath. Once into the hunt, the hunter will calmly be receptive to whatever happens or comes his way. All aspects of the weather are enjoyed to an extent, and simply being outside in the natural world is appreciated. Taking a deer is considered a bonus and not a necessary step to call the day in the woods a success.

All four stages have their pros and cons, and some deer hunters say that they are somewhere between two of the stages. Most popular is between stages three and four.

As an outdoor journalist, it's my responsibility to report the news as honestly and ethically as possible. Being an outdoor journalist also reveals to me a broad outlook of the state of hunting in Ohio and beyond. Spending an hour at a deer checking station during gun season exposes some real truths about our hunting past, present and future. I've seen hundreds of great scenes of father and son, father and daughter, mother and son and numerous relation combinations and nonrelated hunting duos, such as a senior hunter

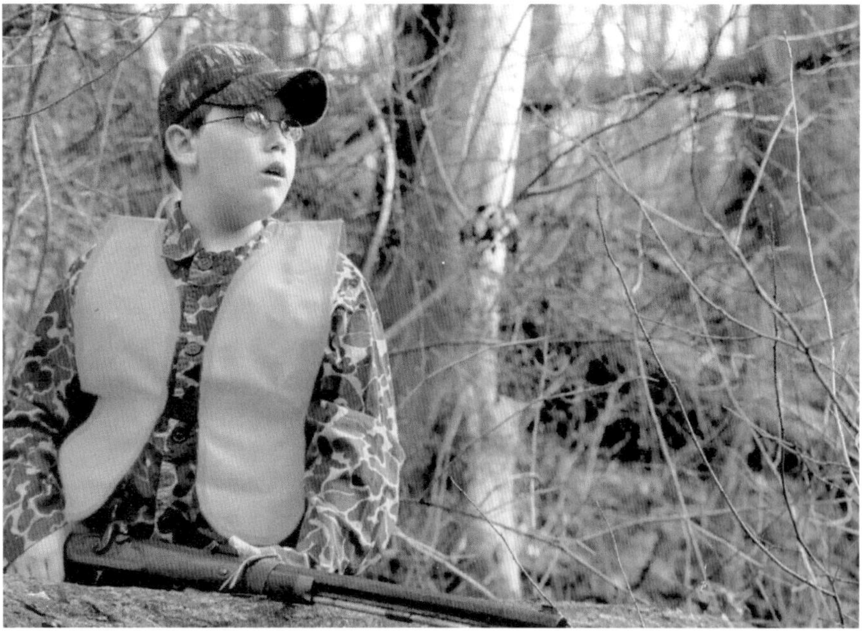

The author's son with a muzzleloading rifle, experiencing deer hunting as generations did a century ago. *Robert Loewendick.*

mentoring a young neighbor on their first deer hunting experience. One statement I hear often at deer checking stations while having a look at a deer just arriving at the station is "Oh it's just a doe." When it comes from a young hunter, I quickly reassure them that their doe is a fine harvest and not simply just a doe. Our culture is stricken with the "bigger is better" attitude in many aspects. The hunting community will be much better off if it avoids that mentality and promotes the reality that all deer are valuable in one way or another.

The thrill of introducing a young person to deer hunting will remain for thousands of veteran deer hunters in every region of Ohio, as it was for them when they got their start. The desire for young people to become a part of Ohio's deer hunting heritage will remain, with decades of deer hunting traditions fueling the extensive efforts. Deer hunters who were a part of the seasons transpiring in the 1950s and on probably understand the most among anyone the importance for encouraging kids to attend a Hunter Education Course and become a licensed hunter. Generations of deer hunters are well anchored throughout Ohio, which grew stronger as the deer herd became better anchored in the state. The next generations of Ohio's deer hunters have the resources and a quality herd of great quantity to continue building a deer hunting legacy like no other.

AFTERWORD

Ohio's turnaround of its white-tailed deer herd is remarkable. It would be interesting to hear what the people who had the vision of bringing back deer to the Buckeye State in the 1920s and 1930s would have to say today. I bet they would find it hard to believe that the few deer they rounded up and delivered to southern Ohio in crates would become a major factor in growing a deer herd of more than 600,000. Many lessons have been taken from the century of evolving deer management goals and practices, some of which are still considered in modern wildlife management planning.

Ohio's deer are no longer a sight for hunters to see while searching deep forests and remote meadows. In many municipalities, deer have become a nuisance. Because of this, special hunts are implemented to reduce the deer's presence to an acceptable level. Again, can you imagine what the earliest wildlife managers would think about the deer herd infiltrating towns and villages on a regular basis? Although, on the other side of that coin are the faces of thousands of wildlife enthusiasts who get some pleasure from having the deer so easily available for viewing.

Deer have been the source of storytelling in North America for centuries. Ohio has a deer legacy that is worth telling about well into the future. Hunting deer with my father was a treasured time in my life, especially now that he is no longer living. My deer hunting now usually involves time with my children. The cycle of hunting traditions continues for thousands of hunters, just as it has for centuries. Although Ohio's deer have had population-affecting events causing their disappearance and then their return, Ohio's deer hunters have maintained their celebrated deer hunting heritage, which will continue into the future.

BIBLIOGRAPHY

Buckeye Big Buck Club. www.buckeyebigbuckclub.org/home.html.

Carskadden, Jeff, and James Morton. *Where the Frolics and War Dances are Held*. Baltimore, MD: Gateway Press, Inc., 1997.

Nagel, James, and Richard Helwig. *The Ohio Hunter.* 1866. *Farmland News*, Archbold, Ohio. The frontier life of Samuel E. Edwards and the columns that appeared in *Farmland News* were compiled and annotated by James Nagel and Richard Helwig.

Ohio Historical Society. www.ohiohistorycentral.org.

Ohio Department of Natural Resources. www.ohiodnr.com.

Putnam County Historical Society. *Reproduction of Putnam County Pioneer Reminiscences. Number One 1878 and Number Two 1887.* Kalida, OH: Whipporwill Publications. 1981.

Reynolds, Mike. "The Theodore Roosevelt Game Preserve—Ohio's first public hunting area." *Wild Ohio Magazine* (Fall 2004). ODNR's Division of Wildlife.

ABOUT THE AUTHOR

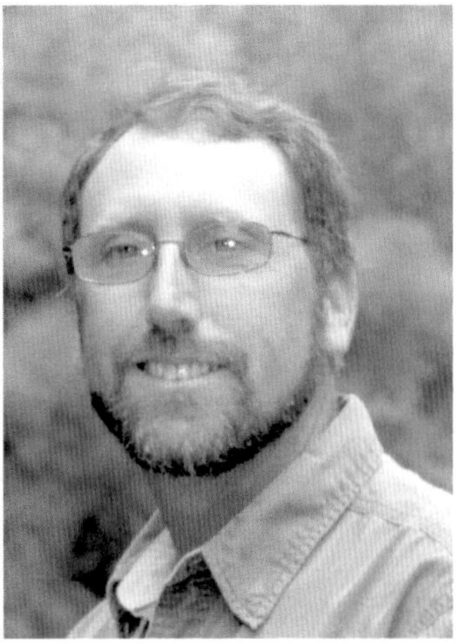

Robert Loewendick is a freelance outdoor writer with work regularly published in magazines, newspapers and on the Internet, both in the United States and worldwide. His award-winning writing has earned him active memberships in Outdoor Writers Association of America and Outdoor Writers of Ohio. Along with Robert's passion for the outdoors is his enthusiasm for writing and photographing the outdoors. Robert believes that if one person, especially a child, is encouraged to spend a day in the outdoors because of his writing, his work will have been successful. While growing up in east-central Ohio, Robert was introduced to the benefits and privileges found in the forests, fields and on the water by his father. For nearly four decades, Robert has traveled the United States and been involved in outdoor pursuits, but the hundreds of days focused on hunting the white-tailed deer were experienced in the Buckeye State.